PRAISE FOR *I CAN ONLY IMAGINE*

"In *I Can Only Imagine*, we are reminded that God is able to transform an abusive and monstrous father into a tenderhearted friend and role model. He is able to change a reluctant choir student into a world-renowned vocalist. And he can turn a song written in ten minutes into an anthem about the wonder of eternity.

"God is able to do 'immeasurably more than all we ask or imagine,' and Bart's story is a testament to that truth. What does God have in store next for his music, his family, his career, and his legacy? The answer's in the title."

—Pastor Greg Laurie

"Bart is a friend of mine. He's the same guy on the surface as he is a thousand feet deep. He knows how to play music, but even more important, he knows how to live life. This isn't a book about Bart; it's about Jesus. It's an invitation to grab your knees and do a cannonball into the big life God promised us if we'll risk being real enough to try."

—Bob Goff
Author, *New York Times*
bestseller *Love Does*

"This book is appropriate because not only does Bart have a song to share but he has a story to tell. I have literally watched the pages of this book play out with Bart as he searched for his identity as a worship leader. He temporarily mistook his identity as the lead singer of MercyMe. Now he is writing, singing, and telling his story about his true identity in Jesus Christ. This book can greatly impact people who experience trials and are searching for their identity."

—Rusty Kennedy
Director, Leavener

I CAN
ONLY
IMAGINE

a Memoir

Bart Millard

WITH ROBERT NOLAND

W PUBLISHING GROUP

AN IMPRINT OF THOMAS NELSON

I Can Only Imagine

© 2018 Bart Millard

Published in Nashville, Tennessee, by W Publishing, an imprint of Thomas Nelson.

Published in association with the literary agency of WTA Services, LLC, Franklin, Tennessee.

Thomas Nelson titles may be purchased in bulk for educational, business, fundraising, or sales promotional use. For information, please e-mail SpecialMarkets@ ThomasNelson.com.

I CAN ONLY IMAGINE is a trademark of MercyMe Music, Inc. Used by permission.

Unless otherwise noted, all Scripture references are taken from the Holy Bible, New International Version˚, NIV˚. Copyright © 1973, 1978, 1984, 2011 by Biblica, Inc.™ Used by permission of Zondervan. All rights reserved worldwide. www.zondervan .com. The "NIV" and "New International Version" are trademarks registered in the United States Patent and Trademark Office by Biblica, Inc.™

Scripture references marked THE MESSAGE are taken from *The Message*. Copyright © 1993, 1994, 1995, 1996, 2000, 2001, 2002 by Eugene H. Peterson. Used by permission of NavPress. All rights reserved. Represented by Tyndale House Publishers, Inc.

Scripture references marked NLT are taken from the Holy Bible, New Living Translation. Copyright © 1996, 2004, 2007, 2013, 2015 by Tyndale House Foundation. Used by permission of Tyndale House Publishers, Inc., Carol Stream, Illinois 60188. All rights reserved.

Any Internet addresses, phone numbers, or company or product information printed in this book are offered as a resource and are not intended in any way to be or to imply an endorsement by Thomas Nelson, nor does Thomas Nelson vouch for the existence, content, or services of these sites, phone numbers, companies, or products beyond the life of this book.

ISBN 978-0-7852-1675-9 (eBook)
ISBN 978-0-7852-1673-5 (TP)

Library of Congress Cataloging-in-Publication Data

Library of Congress Control Number: 2017917450

Printed in the United States of America

18 19 20 21 22   LSC   10 9 8 7 6 5 4 3 2 1

To Shannon, Sam, Gracie, Charlie, Sophie, and Miles.
I know what I was, and I know what I am now.

CONTENTS

AUTHOR'S NOTE

MercyMe!
A Movie and Memoir

Having your life made into a movie is a surreal experience. When the film *I Can Only Imagine* went into production, I quickly learned what an incredible challenge it is to compress a person's life story into less than two hours of screen time. And because movies are so expensive to produce and market, add to that time crunch an intense pressure to make every minute engaging and entertaining for the audience. As I said, it's an incredible challenge.

Storytelling in film is most certainly an art form. Every second counts—literally. After shooting countless hours of footage on location, the very first cut of the film was around six hours long. The directors began by editing the scenes into chronological order in order to tell the story, but because no one had signed on to produce a lengthy TV series docudrama, more than four hours—about two-thirds—of the footage fell to the cutting room floor, as they say. Years had to be edited down to a five-minute composite. A series of events had to be accurately depicted by a single scene. This,

I learned, is why you sometimes hear of a certain actor being cast in a movie and then find out later he or she was edited out or the vast majority of the actor's scenes were deleted.

Given these constraints, the filmmakers did an incredible job of not only producing an amazing movie but also telling my story with authenticity and integrity. Dennis Quaid, the legendary actor who has played a myriad of characters onscreen over the years, played my dad. He really helped me understand why and how to draw the line between the reality of my life and the movie about my life. (I'm forever grateful to Dennis for the time we spent talking about my relationship with my dad between takes.)

So when the opportunity to write my memoir came up in connection with the film, I was really excited to have the opportunity to tell some of the details that couldn't make it into the movie. The filmmakers were locked into an industry time frame, but within these pages, we don't have to be. Now I get to share more about the amazing people who are such a vital part of my story.

I pray you enjoy reading about the roller-coaster ride of my life. But more than anything, I pray that through this book, you will come to know, or know more intimately, the God who offers us a life that is more than we could ever ask for or imagine (Ephesians 3:20).

INTRODUCTION

How Great Is Your Love

> *My heart is steadfast of God,*
> *And I will sing,*
> *With all my heart and soul,*
> *Music for the King.*
> —MERCYME, "HOW GREAT IS YOUR LOVE,"
> FROM *ALMOST THERE* (2001)*

I was standing just offstage at the iconic Ryman Auditorium, Nashville's "Mother Church of Country Music," listening to an incredible band play the intro to my song. The grin on my face was quite literally ear to ear. This was, without a doubt, the single greatest moment of my professional life. All the countless nights I had lain awake envisioning better days and a brighter future, and now this reality I was experiencing outdid them all. I was frightened, but ecstatic. Nervous, yet peaceful. Proud, while humbled.

---

* Words and music by MercyMe. Copyright © 2001 Simpleville Music (ASCAP). All rights reserved. Used by permission.

For the first time *ever* in my life, reality was outrunning my imagination.

And then, just when I thought it couldn't get any better, the crowned "Queen of Christian Pop," Amy Grant, who had been my absolute hero and guiding light from the seventh grade on, stepped up to the microphone. In her angelic, soothing style, she sang the words:

I can only imagine what it will be like . . .

I soaked in the moment, every word and every note. As Amy was finishing the first chorus, it was my cue. Just as we had planned, I stepped out onto the stage, into the spotlight, and into a surreal moment. I walked to the mic, stared out into the sea of faces, drew in the deepest breath I think I've ever taken, and sang,

I can only imagine when that day comes . . .

As I ended the verse and went into the chorus, Amy joined me, along with her husband, Vince Gill, the legendary country music superstar. And then some sort of holy convergence occurred. The crowd gathered there at the Ryman seemed to fade away, and I began to sing for an audience of only two. I envisioned my dad watching, smiling, taking in all that he had prayed for and believed for me, while my heavenly Father was also watching, smiling, accepting my offering of giving Him the glory He so richly deserved.

The acoustics in that hall are like nowhere else in the world, but there was something much bigger happening, something sacred. In this historic sanctuary, once called the Union Gospel Tabernacle, the Reverend Sam Jones used to stand Sunday after Sunday to preach about heaven. Now I stood beside Amy Grant on that legendary stage, singing about the day when we will see Jesus face-to-face. It was an amazing and intimate time of worship as I reflected on all God had done and brought me through to lead me to this moment.

As the crescendo of the last chorus cascaded down over us all and the final chord faded, people applauded and cheered. Amy embraced me as if she were a proud big sister. It was truly a divine hour of blessing rising out of my broken world.

Later that night, alone with my wife, Shannon, I could no longer hold back the tears. God had actually allowed my wildest dreams to come true. But that was just the beginning of the ride of our lives. And it's been one crazy journey, to say the least.

While it has often been a hard road to travel—and, honestly, the success sometimes only made it harder—one thing I know for certain is that the gospel is more alive to me today than ever, thanks to the front-row seat I was given to watch Jesus change my dad.

From a feared monster to a faithful mentor.

From an abusive dad to a loving father.

From a heart of stone to a life of grace.

As Shannon and I continued to share our hearts that night, we thought back to the first time I sat down to visit with Amy about "I Can Only Imagine." The fact that a song I had written moved her and touched her deeply was, well, more than humbling. After all, she'd been singing to me for years through my headphones, helping me through my own hard times.

Amy had asked me where the song came from. It was a mystery even to me how quickly I'd written the song when so many others had been much more difficult to write. I told her the truth: "It just kind of happened. Lyrics took about ten minutes, I guess. Music took about the same."

Thoughtfully, graciously, out of a heart of wisdom and life experience, she said, "Bart, you didn't write that song in ten minutes. It took a lifetime."

Amy was absolutely right. "Imagine" had been coming to me throughout my entire existence—arriving as a divine appointment at a spiritual crossroads of life and art. In moments of pain, confusion, and despair, God had been writing the words on my heart, slowly giving them genesis in the chaos of my life. And in every instance when I experienced His peace, love, and joy, the chorus was being shaped and sung into my spirit, the melody intertwining through my days like an unending thread weaving together the patchwork of a cherished family heirloom quilt.

But the fruit on a tree's branches is not grown for the tree but for those who will eat from it. Although this song may have been written *from* my life, it was *for* anyone who would "taste and see that the LORD is good" (Psalm 34:8). King David, one of the most prolific songwriters in history, proclaimed to God, "I'll be the poet who sings your glory—and live what I sing every day" (Psalm 61:8 THE MESSAGE).

So, echoing that same spirit, this is the story behind my song.

One

DEAR YOUNGER ME

*Of all the painful memories still running through my
head,
I wonder how much different things would be,
Dear younger me.*

—MercyMe, "Dear Younger Me," from
Welcome to the New (2014)*

My dad was Arthur Millard Jr., son of Arthur Millard Sr. When Dad
was around ten years old, and his brother, Mike, was about seven, my
grandfather left the family, divorced my grandmother, and quickly
remarried. Because of Arthur Sr.'s devastating choices, my dad took
on the immense pressure of suddenly being head of the household,
a horribly premature responsibility that birthed an anger and bitterness in his heart that would affect him throughout his life.

As a young man, my father was a star football player at Greenville High School. Greenville is a small town in Texas, about forty-five miles northeast of Dallas. He became an All-American at the position of center. For you non-sports folks, that is the player in the middle of the offensive line who snaps the football to the quarterback, then blocks the defense away from the man with the ball. Needless to say, guys who play center are big, tough dudes, brutes you do not want to mess with or make angry. My dad was no exception.

He was offered football scholarships to several schools, but by the time Dad graduated from high school in 1961, he chose Southern Methodist University in Dallas so he could stay close to home. Another important factor in this decision was that he was dating a young lady named Adele. Adele, known to her family and friends as Dell, would eventually become my mom. She was the daughter of a pastor who had planted a new church in Greenville.

When a Dream Dies

By his sophomore year in college, Dad was playing center for the SMU Mustangs and had dreams of going on to play pro football. But with all the time and energy demanded by his sports schedule, coupled with a full slate of classes, he deeply missed his sweetheart, Dell. He also struggled with a strong sense of responsibility to take care of his mom, so Dad made the difficult decision to let go of his dream, leave school, and move back home.

From that day when he drove away from SMU's campus back into Greenville's city limits, Dad never lived anywhere else and rarely ever left town. He and my mom soon married, and, in 1968, they welcomed their first child, Stephen. Once again, Dad had the responsibility of supporting a family.

The decision to walk away from his opportunity to play football would haunt my dad for a very long time, and a deep regret festered in him, eventually turning into a cancerous case of the what-ifs. As a result, sports were a constant focus in our family, and soon that near-obsession demanded that my brother and I get involved too. Whenever Stephen and I were playing sports, things were always a little better at home.

Several years after leaving SMU, Dad got together with some of his old teammates. They told him that the Green Bay Packers and the Baltimore Colts had been considering him in the draft, but when he quit college ball, he fell off both teams' radars. Evidently, he had never known that possibility was forming behind the scenes. That kind of information can be hard for any man to take, especially when disappointment is already a constant companion. This was one of many little slices of life that caused my dad to become a realist, always insisting that people have to give up their dreams to have any sort of family stability.

So many people have told me over the years how in that season of his life, when he had just come home from college, Dad was a "big ol' teddy bear." Everybody liked Arthur and wanted to be his friend. In the Greenville area, he was the local sports hero, popular everywhere he went. Dad was the proverbial "big fish in a small pond," which can be a blessing but also a curse, because fish live in glass houses.

My mom tells me that back then, he was the greatest guy you could ever know. But that was before I was born.

Waking Up in a Different World

In order to make a dependable living for his new family, Dad got a job with the Texas Highway Department. The Lone Star State

3

has long been fiscally solid, so stability, pay, and benefits were all available for their workers, from new hires straight up the steps of the organizational ladder to retirement. When he first started, Dad was a flagman, directing traffic in construction zones. While this job may look like a boring one, it is actually quite dangerous because of the necessity of being in such close proximity to the traffic.

One particular day in 1969, as he was flagging cars, a driver in a diesel truck struck Dad, launching him at least fifty feet into the air and knocking him unconscious. After the ambulance took him to the hospital and the doctors had run a gamut of tests, they told Mom that, miraculously, he had no broken bones, but he was in a coma and the prognosis was uncertain.

There were many days when Mom prepared herself that he would not make it through. But to say my father was tough would be an understatement. He was always a fighter.

It's likely that he had some sort of brain trauma, possibly a major frontal lobe injury. No one has ever been completely certain. And, of course, he'd played at a high level of football for years, likely suffering repeated concussions, way before these issues were ever on the radar of coaches and trainers. This was also before the invention of MRIs and the sophisticated equipment available today, so the exact details and state of Dad's medical issues went undetected and untreated.

To everyone's surprise, Dad regained consciousness eight weeks after the accident. But he woke up in a different world and in a different life, with a new personality, an altered state of thinking. He was not the same man who'd been Greenville's favorite son.

Family members and a few friends told me that when my dad woke from the coma, he was a monster. The teddy bear of days past had become a grizzly. He had to be restrained in the hospital bed. It took several orderlies to hold him down. He was incredibly strong, which gave his anger so much more to work with. A guy who could manhandle college varsity linebackers had no problem overpowering a few nurses, regardless of their gender or size. Even his attitude and mouth were affected. He was crude and rude with the nurses, something he would never have done before.

Mom said my dad never showed any temper before the accident, except for occasionally on the football field. He never even raised his voice. The family doctor who delivered me was the physician treating him, and to this day he tells me how different Dad was before the accident.

But the new Arthur Millard Jr. was the only one I would know for the first fifteen years of my life.

The husband my mom took home from the hospital was not the one who had left for work on that fateful morning just two months prior, and the day he was discharged began the countdown to Mom leaving him. Anger and rage moved into their home and became permanent residents. But, oddly, when Dad was out in public, he managed to keep it all in check and hide it from everyone who loved the local football hero. Who knows? Maybe people *did* see the change in him but just looked the other way to not get involved. After all, that's the small-town way—mind your own business while staying in everyone else's.

Our house had that classic 1960s front sitting room, the place you kept immaculate and never touched, just in case the pastor or some other local VIP dropped by. It was the one room that looked like June Cleaver's or Aunt Bea's entire house, and Mom would do everything in her power to keep visitors there so as to *not* see that the rest of our home was a wreck. That space was a metaphor for my family's life: the immaculate and perfect setting we allowed everyone to see, while the rest of the house was kept private and isolated from view. Where we actually lived became a mess that none of us knew how to clean up. So no one ever did, and then it was too late.

For example, Mom said that one day she came home from shopping alone and Dad asked her who she had been with. She told him no one. But possessive paranoia got the best of him, and he launched into a rant and berated her, accusing her of lying and cheating.

Now, my mom was what I would call a lady's lady. She always looked her absolute best and enjoyed nice dresses and jewelry. In moments like this, while Dad wouldn't touch her, he would go get one of her best necklaces—anything he knew she enjoyed or was precious to Mom—and rip it apart right in front of her as a form of punishment. Then he'd leave the pieces on the floor and walk away in a huff.

Jealous rage became a regular event at our house. My mom stayed afraid for her life until the day she left—and even some days afterward. It was definitely a Jekyll-and-Hyde story. Was Dad's behavior due to a brain injury or chemical imbalance caused by the accident, or was he just a tortured soul because of his own family's broken past? We'll never know.

By the way, just to be clear, he never drank alcohol. No drugs. The fire of Dad's anger never needed any such fuel. Who knows what may have happened if he had resorted to any of those vices?

Those closest to Mom would have understood if she had left Dad much sooner, though back in that day such a decision was not at all common. I think she stuck around as long as she did and endured all she could because she truly believed the man she fell in love with and married was still in there . . . somewhere.

Years ago I saw the movie *Regarding Henry*, starring Harrison Ford. It's the fictional tale of a narcissistic, wealthy surgeon who gets shot in the head during a robbery and, due to the injury, becomes very childlike and loving—the opposite of who he had been before. The point of the movie was that the tragedy actually saved his personal life. I remember thinking how the truck that hit Dad was like that movie gunshot, except the plot was flipped. Dad's tragedy devastated his life.

But my father's script was still being written, and there was much more plot in God's pen.

Ready or Not, Here I Come!

In the midst of all this madness, Mom became pregnant with me. On December 1, 1972, I came into the world: Bart Marshall Millard, named after the legendary Packers quarterback, Bart Starr. (So why isn't my middle name Starr?) Likely my dad was hoping I would be the football savior of the family, so he decided to kick this kid off right with a proper namesake.

In spite of my name, Dad decided he already had the sports-buddy son in Stephen, and he didn't need another one. Plus, it didn't help that I was a mama's boy who often cried when she wasn't around. As I became a mischievous toddler, my spankings slowly escalated from normal discipline to verbal and physical abuse. I would eventually become his only target.

One day, in a single conversation, everything changed for my family. Not in any sort of heated argument at all, out of nowhere Dad popped off with, "Dell, why don't you just get the hell out?" Mom saw that backhanded question as his permission for her to leave. So she told him she would do just that. And she followed through with Dad's hateful suggestion.

I often wonder how many times she had decided to leave, only to break down and give him another shot. All too often, you hear of women in these circumstances being horribly hurt or even dying because of the just-one-more-chance syndrome. Regardless, this time she told my dad that she was leaving and taking Stephen and me with her. I was three years old.

One of the first vivid childhood memories I have is of the day we moved out. Not at all understanding the depth of what was actually happening, I helped Mom carry whatever I could manage at my young age out to the car. Dad just sat in his living room chair the entire time, staring forward, prideful, acting stoic, appearing to ignore that his life was coming apart at the seams. It's so strange how arrogance can convince people not to lift a finger to try to stop the reality that they are losing everything.

I remember him asking me in a sarcastic tone, "Where are you going with my stuff, boy?" That's a confusing question for a toddler, especially when you're just carrying your toys to the car.

Broken Home, Broken Hearts

Very few people knew how much my dad had changed after his accident, because our family kept this intense and volatile fact a secret. So when Mom left my dad, she became the one at whom everyone would point the finger. Everyone loved Arthur Millard Jr., and this was small-town USA. Public opinion was that my mom was the problem. People assumed she had done something wrong or had chosen to leave for no good reason, which of course was not true. Everyone thought if Arthur had been at fault, then he would have been the one to go. But he was staying in the house, and she was apparently moving out on her own accord. Folks said, "How bad can it be, Dell? Why don't you just grin and bear it? Just stick it out."

Often when private problems become public knowledge, people

make a lot of poor assumptions and ask all the wrong questions. The age-old clichés and social lessons that we all must be reminded of, even today, is to never judge a book by its cover and also not to speak ill against others until you have walked a mile in their shoes. My mom didn't speak up to defend herself because she felt no one would believe her.

At some point in all this drama, Mom filed for divorce. When we left Dad and moved into a rental house, a deep depression overcame her. She may have escaped the fear, but she walked right into a hopeless life. She still loved Dad and wanted so badly for her marriage to work. Mom just wanted back the man she'd married, the husband she'd had before the accident.

Struggling with her new life, Mom often wouldn't get out of bed when she didn't have to be at work. My brother and I had to fend for and feed ourselves, as well as take care of each other the best we could. We would even tuck her in at night and then be on our own. She rarely cooked, so she would bring home fast food. I have distinct memories of sitting in the living room, eating Taco Bell, and watching the evening sitcoms on TV.

While that may sound awesome for an occasional binge, believe me, it's not that great on a regular basis. But it was the best Mom could do under the circumstances. Stephen and I ate a *lot* of toast, one of the only "meals" a little kid can fix. We also figured out that if we could get canned food open, we could eat it as is.

This was our new reality: a single mom who felt forced out into life with two young boys, struggling to survive. Life was tough for us all.

Sometimes when Mom was gone to work, out running errands, or still in bed, Stephen and I would get hungry with no food in the house, and we would call our grandmothers, who lived nearby. One of them would either bring us a meal or come get us and take us to her house. During this season we spent a lot of nights at one of their homes. Both were strong Christian women who provided stability for us when we needed it most.

When I was just beginning to talk, I started calling both of my grandmothers by the name of Mammaw. I wasn't yet able to distinguish them by different names, so, as is often the case with grandkids and their grandparents, their new names were at the mercy of the strange pronunciation of a toddler. So there was Mammaw Lindsey, Mom's mom, who was the godliest woman I ever knew, and then Mammaw Millard, Dad's mom, who was the funniest woman I ever knew. (She was godly, too, but super comical.) Thank the Lord for the prayers and provision of grandmas! I'm not sure what would have happened to Stephen and me without those two sweet saints being the constants in our lives.

Even though we saw my dad and he had custody of us every other weekend, he would sometimes drive by Mom's house, yell out, and ridicule her for leaving him. He would call our home phone and do the same. This only increased the fear.

Anytime Dad would upset or scare me, I would cry and ask for Mom, especially when we were with him for the entire weekend. One time when I was in third grade, I started bawling and calling for her. Dad would normally just yell at me and tell me to stop. But on this one occasion, he started crying and told me that he missed her too. In later years, I would see this was much more of the deep truth in Dad's heart than any of us ever realized.

Eventually, Mom started dating again. I have an early memory of the explosive level of my dad's violent temper from around the time when she was just starting to date Gary, her first boyfriend after the divorce. Gary had spanked me once, and when Dad found out, he filed that little detail away for when he saw him again.

Dad came to pick Stephen and me up from Mom's house, and

Gary arrived around the same time. As Mom's new guy came up the stairs to her house, Dad grabbed him, threw him onto the hood of Gary's own car, and said, "If you ever lay a hand on either of my boys again, I will rip your throat out." I remember the shock of watching that happen. As we drove away, Gary just lay there on the hood. I didn't think he was dead, but I never saw him move either.

Fairly soon after, Mom married Gary. He had children from a previous marriage, and when his kids came to stay with them, Stephen and I went to our dad's. But it turned out that Gary was an alcoholic, and when he was drunk, he beat my mom. One time Mom came to pick us up from my dad's with her arm in a cast. She told Dad that she had slipped on the sidewalk during the recent ice storm and broken it, but he knew that wasn't true. I guess you could say that Mom had jumped from Arthur's frying pan into Gary's fire. She most definitely was getting burned everywhere.

Mom quickly realized she had made a huge mistake and couldn't risk another violent relationship, so she and Gary divorced just a few months into the marriage. So now she was alone once again.

I really think that Mom was just looking for someone to take care of her, and she thought that being with the wrong guy was better than being by herself. She so wanted the knight in shining armor on the white horse to come and save her, but she just kept getting the end of the sword.

Following what was now her second divorce in a short time, Mom's depression grew worse. Easily irritated by all the typical questions and demands of children, she developed a short fuse with Stephen and me. Through all the chaos, my brother and I just kept taking care of each other, under the watchful eye of our grandmothers.

The One Left Behind

When I was eight years old, Mom married her third husband, Lawrence. He was a good man; Mom really loved him, and he loved her. But his company told him he had to transfer from Dallas to San Antonio, and there was considerable pressure on Mom for my brother and me to stay in Greenville. Everyone seemed to think that Stephen and I needed to have the "stability" of staying in the same town, same school, and same home, with extended family close by for help. Dad told Mom, "Not that long ago, you were getting beat up by your husband, and now you want to take off with the boys and this new guy I don't even know. I think they need to stay right here with me."

For Stephen, this wasn't such a bad deal. He was fine to stay in Greenville and live with Dad, because now that he was in his teens, more independent, and really into sports, they got along well. For me, well, that was a very different story. With Dad's temper focused on me, I felt much safer with my mom. But she had to leave with her new husband, and Dad convinced her that my brother and I had to stay.

Everyone in the family knew what had been decided—except me.

Mom packed all of Stephen's and my stuff into her car. She told me we were going to Dad's house. When we arrived, she and Dad took all our things into the house. I started asking what was going on. Stephen, of course, was old enough to understand and was already aware of what was about to take place.

Outside the back door of Dad's house, my mom knelt down and explained to me that she had to go away and I had to stay behind. Crying, she hugged me, told me she loved me, and then got in the car to drive away.

Devastated is not a big enough word to describe what it felt like to be eight years old and watch your mom leave you. In that moment, my world crashed down around me. I felt as though the ground had reached up and swallowed me.

I tried running after the car, crying out for her not to leave, but I eventually gave up and stopped on the road. I still recall seeing the glimmering metal on the bumper through the blur of my tears as she drove away. The heat waves from the blazing Texas sun danced off the access road in front of our house, distorting the image of her car as it disappeared into the distance.

She was gone. I felt so alone.

As my mom drove out of my life, rejection moved into my heart.

For what seemed like forever, I stood at the back door of our house, crying hysterically, repeating "I'm sorry" over and over for whatever I had done to give Mom a reason to make this horrible decision. I didn't know about how family pressure had forced her to accept this outcome, or that she was just as heartbroken as I was. I couldn't have possibly comprehended all that adult drama.

They say leaving those you love is the hardest thing you can ever do, but I would contest that it's much harder if you're the child who is the one left behind. When parents leave, kids can't understand anything other than the thought that *Mom or Dad must have left because of me*. I *know* that. Firsthand.

Dad and Stephen sat in the house just listening to me wail. My mom hadn't actually abandoned me forever, but it didn't matter. I *felt* abandoned. Whatever the truth was, all I knew was that my heart was ripped apart that day.

Two

THE HURT AND THE HEALER

It's the moment when humanity
Is overcome by majesty,
When grace is ushered in for good,
And all our scars are understood.

—MERCYME, "THE HURT & THE HEALER,"
FROM THE ALBUM OF THE SAME NAME (2012)*

My mom moved six hours away, but it seemed more like halfway around the world to a kid who had rarely gone outside the city limits. And it may as well have been, because for several years I saw her only on certain holidays and occasional scheduled visits. For a very long time, I held on to the hope that my parents would eventually get back together, but Stephen never did. Our five-year difference in age, coupled with his ability to understand the nature of Mom leaving, gave my brother and me very different perspectives of the family's future.

With Dad's modest income from the highway department, we lived in a typical middle-class neighborhood in a small, unassuming house. Built in the early sixties and featuring the classic avocado-green appliances and wood-grain paneling, it was the only home I ever knew, located right off a major highway on the frontage road. At the time, I never considered us to be poor, but we were certainly way closer to that end of the economic spectrum compared to most other people I knew.

I grew up in the pre-video-game generation, and TV wasn't really on my radar. With just three or four stations to choose from, picked up by the rabbit-ears antenna, television offered nothing for kids except maybe an hour after school and three hours of Saturday morning cartoons. My imagination wrote way better scripts anyway, sometimes playing out several complete episodes of adventure in a single afternoon after I got home from school.

The hit TV series *The Wonder Years*, which was about suburban life in the late 1960s and early 1970s, featured a dad; the older brother, Wayne; and the younger brother, Kevin. These characters were a fairly accurate picture of Dad, Stephen, and me when I was growing up. The age differences, personalities, attitudes, and issues on that show mirrored those of the three Millard males living under the same roof—although I don't think I would call my childhood years a "wonder."

Stephen and I had the classic older-brother, kid-brother relationship, in that he could pester and punch me all he wanted to make my life miserable—but if anyone else said anything bad about me or did anything to me, he would quickly jump to my defense. One time, for example, after I had come back from Mom's in San Antonio, one of his buddies popped off and said something about her not wanting me. I thought Stephen was going to kill the guy. He knew my weak spots and wouldn't let anyone hurt me—and he would make them pay if they tried. No one knew what we had had to endure better than we did.

After Mom left for San Antonio and it was clear that life was now just the three of us, Dad's anger focused completely on me. I started receiving the brunt of his rage, and spankings turned into whippings. He grew more comfortable and more frequent with his violence toward me. Even Mammaw Millard, the family member closest to us, who knew Dad had a temper and was a tough disciplinarian, never suspected the levels to which he was going with me. And Stephen and I certainly weren't going to tell *anyone* because of what Dad might do. Without Mom around as the other parent, there was no longer any accountability and no one to tell him he was taking things too far or it was time to stop. No one except me, of course, but he didn't hear me any longer.

The family secret of abuse not only continued but was now being driven deeper.

The Original Escape Game

The world inside a kid's imagination is often the only means of relief from a hostile environment. With an absentee mom, a brother who was now a busy teenager, and an emotionally disengaged dad, I was Andy in the movie *Toy Story*—the kid playing alone in his room for hours upon hours, acting out all manner of tales and adventures. I would set up elaborate sets in my room and play out every scenario my creativity could conjure. With simple, inexpensive, often homemade and handmade toys, I built all kinds of strange contraptions in an attempt to break away from the reality of my home life.

The vast landscape within my mind was my constant and immediate escape. In the blink of an eye, I could blast off to another planet or sail away to an uncharted island sanctuary. I also began drawing and became consumed with my sketchbook. Honestly, I would exercise *any* creativity I could to try to express what was built up in my heart that could never seem to find its way out.

I was also Max in the classic book *Where the Wild Things Are*. While I didn't own a wolf suit like the kid in the story, I saw Dad as the worst sort of monster living in my world. In my sketchpad, I often drew myself in different scenes with a large, two-horned, hairy ogre.

During this season of my life, music also started to take hold of me and offer temporary but welcomed respites from reality. I remember we had an 8-track tape player (a pre-cassette format) that had a radio in the same unit. You could tune in to a station, hit Record on the 8-track, and "tape" the radio show you were listening to. I loved the band Electric Light Orchestra, who had hit after hit back in those days. My favorite vocalist was Leo Sayer (and he's still high on my list today). His *Endless Flight* album from 1976 is still amazing! One night I recorded Casey Kasem's radio show *American Top 40*, and then I wore out the 8-track by playing the recording constantly, getting lost in the words of the pop songs of the early 1980s. I can still hear Casey's program ending with his famous catchphrase: "Keep your feet on the ground and keep reaching for the stars."

Music became my ultimate escape, one I have never outgrown.

Running the Gauntlet

Dad had both a leather strap and a wooden paddle with holes in it that cut down on resistance to airflow. At least, I think that's what the holes were for. Supposedly, those made the spanking hurt worse.

If you're anywhere in the neighborhood of, say, forty years old, you probably heard the rumor that your principal had one of these torture devices hidden away in his office for the *really* bad kids. Well, while I'm not sure about our principal, Dad for sure had one.

I could do something as innocent as leave the bread out on the table after a meal or put it back in the wrong place, and he would knock me across the room. I was rarely ever given any real explanation for the punishment, so I often didn't know exactly what set him off. Soon, *everything* seemed to have the potential to get me in trouble, even good things, because I couldn't be sure how Dad would react to anything related to me.

One particular time, when I was in Mrs. Burns's fifth-grade class, the school gave me a letter to take home that said I was an honor student. They asked me to get Dad to sign it and bring it back to the office. Because I felt I couldn't take the chance of the letter being a match to light his fuse, I forged his signature and returned it. Let's just say that my rendition of his name looked nothing like it was supposed to.

The school secretary easily detected the forgery, called my dad, and laughingly told him the office staff thought it was cute that I had tried to fake his signature on something as harmless as an honor roll letter. She thought it was obviously just a silly misunderstanding. Well, Dad didn't think it was very funny. Not only was there no praise for my being on the honor roll, but the forgery punishment was severe. One of his specific triggers was anything that made him appear foolish or feel embarrassed in front of the folks in town.

If Stephen brought home a borderline report card, Dad would tell him he would need to work harder and get better grades. If I brought home the same or better, he would wait until we were alone and then get out the strap. At the time I assumed Dad dealt with

Stephen the same way he dealt with me and that our punishments were kept separate and private. But many years later as adults, when my brother and I started opening up about our childhoods, I realized I had borne the brunt of Dad's abuse.

Still, I always maintained an "I'd rather be safe than sorry" strategy. I scrutinized my every action to avoid getting hit.

The Vicious Cycle

Dad worked hard to make sure Stephen and I grew up in *his* reality, where dreams die and you work every day to just get by. As a result, my creative imagination often conflicted with Dad's commitment to "realism." Many times, in response to some creation I had made or goal I had shared, he would give me a speech that went something like this: "I'm going to teach you something, Bart. Dreams don't pay the bills. Nothing good comes from it. All it does is keep you from all this." His eyes scanned around the house as he spoke with a biting and bitter tone. "Dreams just keep you from knowing what's real . . . You understand that? . . . Huh?"

Full of fear, I would glance up, brace myself for the possibility of things escalating, nod my head, and manage to mutter, "Yes, Daddy."

The only time Dad expressed any sort of love or affection to me was after he had whipped me. Nearly every time, when he had calmed down, he would let me sit on his lap, and we would watch TV together—I guess because he felt bad or guilty. Sometimes he would attempt to explain why he disciplined me and why I needed to obey. While I didn't always understand the severity of the punishment versus the actual crime, I still always savored those moments of normal father-and-son intimacy.

This was a consistent pattern throughout my childhood—a whipping followed by affection. So I associated that a father's closeness only followed severe discipline.

There were times when I hid the strap and the paddle because I was scared and didn't want him to whip me. He would think he forgot where he put them, while I hoped he might cool off by the time he found them. But then there were plenty more times when I so wanted his attention that I intentionally crossed the line just so he would get out the paddle—because I knew that afterward we could then cuddle up and watch TV together.

Sad? Yes. But true.

Suburban Survival

Stephen and I would do pretty much anything to avoid Dad's wrath. When Stephen was a junior in high school, he got a job at a pharmacy in town. He had been late to work several times, and the manager had threatened to fire him if he was late again. One morning, Stephen overslept and woke up an hour late. He knew he was going to get canned, and he knew how mad that would make Dad, so Stephen came up with this crazy scheme that he would tell his boss that he was late because he had been jumped and beaten up. He told me to punch him in the face until the black-and-blue bruises were convincing.

Standing in the middle of our living room, Stephen said, "Okay, hit me, Bart. Hard. Up by my eyes."

I did not want to punch my brother, so I was almost crying, telling him, "No, I can't hit you like that!"

Stephen started shoving me, calling me names, and trying to provoke me to hit him. Finally, I got mad enough, hauled off, and nailed him with my fist. He looked in the mirror and said, "No, that's not enough, Bart. You're going to have to hit me more, and harder!"

Starting to get the hang of my left hook and right jab, I punched Stephen several times around his face until he felt there was enough physical evidence to back up the story to his boss. But then, just to make absolutely certain his face was convincing enough, he decided to get a razor blade and carefully cut a slit near his eye. Yes, he cut himself open and intentionally bled to finish off his I-got-beaten-up story.

Man, what we would go through to keep peace with Dad was crazy.

But there were other side effects of the lack of parental attention. For example, I was never taken to a dentist growing up, and no one ever taught me how to or made me brush my teeth, so by the time I was in high school, they were yellow. Literally, each of my parents assumed the other had taken care of that detail, when in reality, neither had. Because dental hygiene was never put on my radar, the first time I went to a dentist was in the first year of my marriage, when my wife strongly suggested it was time for me to go.

My Mammaw Millard worked at JCPenney, so I would go there to get shoes and clothes that were damaged or returned, ones they couldn't sell or send back to the manufacturer. Because of factors like these, I was an easy target for being made fun of at school. Even though I was named after Bart Starr, the legendary quarterback, kids in a pack can destroy anything. My name rhymes perfectly with a slang word for flatulence, so I was always called Bart the Fart. My saving grace, if you want to call it that, was that I was bigger than most of the other kids in my grade.

But rather than rely on size, I used comedy as my first line of defense. I always worked hard to be funny. Humor got me attention in a wide variety of circles, and I used it to my full advantage.

My brother made fun of me all the time, too, so I got really good at turning on anyone who ridiculed me. I was the king of the cut-down and could go toe-to-toe with anybody.

Affection Deficit Disorder

Because I was constantly starved for affection and did almost any-thing to get it, I preferred my dad beat me rather than ignore me. At least when he was knocking me around, I was the center of atten-tion in his world. Of course, this isn't logical, but this is the way a needy and desperate child thinks.

The worst whipping Dad gave me was also one of the last. It happened right before the end of fifth grade. I don't remember what he thought I had done, but he must have had extra time to grow angry about it as he waited, belt in hand, for me to come home. When I walked through the back door, he came out of nowhere and blindsided me. He whipped me from the middle of my back down to my calves, so by the time he stopped, I had turned several different shades of purple from one side of my body to the other. The stinging on my skin was excruciating. The really bad part of a beating like that is, as the hours go by, the pain just gets worse.

Even the pressure of the elastic band on my underwear hurt, so I lay in bed all night on my stomach, completely naked, with nothing touching my backside. My dad confessed to me many years later that the realization of what he had done to me in his rage hurt him deeply, and he had cried a lot that night. Well, I cried a lot that night, too—from the physical pain. As I so often did, I stuffed down the emotional hurt, adding yet another layer to deal with someday down the road.

Dad called Mom and told her he wanted to send me to San Antonio over the summer and then have me start sixth grade there.

Just me—Stephen wouldn't be going because he was about to start his senior year. My guess is Dad was concerned that the next thing I did might finally push him over the edge, so he decided to ship me off to Mom. She agreed to the arrangement.

Once again, having no choice in the decision, I had to go. But I went kicking and screaming. I hadn't lived with Mom since I was in third grade, and I had only seen her on occasional holiday visits. I went from living with my brother to being an only child. I also quickly decided that I hated my stepdad, Lawrence, Mom's third husband. He wasn't mean to me and actually treated me way better than Dad did. I just didn't like the fact that Mom was married to someone else. I wanted no part of this stepdad business.

Lawrence constantly tried to take me fishing or get me to help him build something because he knew I liked to create. But I would not cooperate. Fishing meant being outdoors in the steaming central Texas summer heat, and I was accustomed to creating things by myself. I also had trouble navigating the concept that a father figure would want to be involved in my life for any good reason. I just couldn't escape the parental paradigm I had always had.

For example, one day Mom and Lawrence started arguing. In my experience, any conflict always escalated into some sort of physical violence. As their voices began to rise in anger, Lawrence took Mom by the arm and told her they needed to go into another room and not fight in front of me. All I could think was that he was going to take her in there to beat her. So I stormed out on the porch and grabbed the first thing I could find that looked like a weapon a sixth grader could use. In the corner stood a wooden boat oar. I grabbed it by the handle and walked back in the house, straight over to Lawrence, who was turned away from me. I hit him as hard as I could across the back of the head. The boat paddle snapped in half, and Lawrence collapsed to the floor.

Mission accomplished. Stepdad neutralized. Mom saved. Bart wins. The crowd roars! (Remember my vivid imagination?)

But Mom did not act like a damsel rescued. She screamed at me, "Bart, what have you done? What were you thinking? You could have killed him!"

I freaked out, realizing I could have actually murdered him.

A few very long minutes later, Lawrence, though still a bit dazed, was on his feet. I cried and told him how sorry I was. After all, he really was a nice guy, and I didn't actually want him to die. I just didn't want to have to live with him.

To his credit, Lawrence told me he understood how it could have looked to me as though he wanted to harm Mom. He knew I was just being protective. To my surprise, he forgave me and let it go. (Whew!)

In Greenville, I had been accustomed to walking or riding my bike all over town. It didn't take me long to get anywhere I wanted to go. But in San Antonio, Mom wouldn't allow me to go more than about a block without telling me she didn't want anyone to hurt or kidnap me. I felt as if I were constantly under house arrest. Unhappiness and loneliness overwhelmed me, and I became depressed. Even though Dad was abusive, he and Stephen were the only family I felt I really knew. I wanted to go back to my old, abnormally normal life. While I was fine living with Mom, I just wanted to be back in my small hometown.

Finally, toward the end of sixth grade, Mom and Dad talked over what was going on with me. In one particular phone call, Dad even voiced that he missed me, and Stephen told me Dad had expressed that to him too.

Maybe Dad had decided things were going to be different between us, but I had already concluded I would risk returning to the abuse rather than live in San Antonio as an only child with an annoying stepdad. So my parents decided I would go back to Greenville as soon as school was out.

That was the last time I lived with Mom.

From Anger to Apathy

Things took an odd turn with Dad not long after I came back from San Antonio. I believe he was hoping that the time away from him and Stephen, and now the chance to have a fresh start, would have helped me grow up some. But soon after I returned, I followed my brother to a party at his friend's house. Everyone there was older than me. A guy had what looked to me like a regular bottle of mouthwash and was challenging people to drink it.

Remember, I was starved for attention. I stepped forward and told everyone that I would take the dare. I was thinking, *Drinking mouthwash can't kill you! What could possibly go wrong?* I'd seize the moment and coolness would follow. (You're shaking your head right now, aren't you?)

Well, the mouthwash bottle was filled with a mixture of peppermint schnapps and Everclear. (A necessary detail here: while both are liquor, Everclear comes in two alcohol volumes: 75.5 percent and 95 percent.) Like some sort of bad excuse for a frat boy, I downed the whole bottle.

The amount I drank should have killed me. My blood alcohol level had to have been in the danger zone, especially for a kid my age and size.

I passed out on a waterbed (remember those?), and eventually—miraculously—I woke up in the middle of the night and joined a group of guys walking home. But we got caught by one of the dads. He drove us back to his house, and we slept it off there.

That situation was one of the countless times God's grace and protection intervened in my life. Somehow, I survived with no harmful or lasting effects.

The next morning, the dad whose house we'd crashed at said, "Bart, your father needs to know what happened last night. Are you going to tell him, or do I need to call him about it?" I assured him that I would tell Dad, so he wouldn't have to go to all that trouble. But I lied. My plan was to not say a word about it—ever.

I thought I had gotten away with it until a few months later. I was going with the same group of friends to the mall in Dallas. When Dad dropped me off at my friend's house, his father came out to the truck and jokingly said, "Hey, Arthur, don't worry. I'll make sure they don't drink like they did last time."

I was so busted.

Dad's demeanor changed immediately, and he told me to get back in the truck. I quietly complied. That was a very, very long drive home. Fortunately, years before, I had calculated exactly how far my dad's arm could reach to the right with his seat belt on, so I sat as close to the window as I possibly could, just in case he decided to get started on me while we were headed home. I knew for sure that when we got back to the house I would get the worst beating of my life.

After we came in the back door, I braced myself for the rage. But Dad, stone-faced and emotionless, just looked at me and calmly stated, "You know what, Bart? I just don't care anymore. You do what you want."

And the crazy thing was—he did exactly what he said. He stopped caring. That very minute.

I'd had a growth spurt the year I had lived with Mom and was now much bigger. I also think that, with the black-and-blue beating still etched in his memory, Dad just gave up. He didn't want to exert the physical, emotional, and mental energy on me, so he officially resigned from parenting.

If I walked in his room and said something like, "Hey, Dad, I'm going to the movies tonight with Kent," he would glare at me and blurt out, "Remember, Bart, I don't care. Do what you want." Over the years, his bitter words aimed my way always sounded like someone with a horrible grudge. He consistently reminded me that he no longer cared what I did, where I went, who I was with, or when I came home.

But even then, I still cared about Dad. He was all I had left. I couldn't afford to *not* care.

As a result of Dad's new parenting style, I could come home in the middle of the night without getting in trouble. There was no curfew. No accountability. No supervision. A lot of my friends said, "Wow, Bart's so lucky. He doesn't have to be home at a certain time or answer to anyone." Little did they know I would have traded all my freedom for the love and care they had from their families.

I took every chance I could to hang out with other people, especially to be around loving parents. I never liked being alone, because I was already by myself so much of the time. I would go to friends' houses and stay as long as they would let me. The only warning Dad would ever offer was, "Don't wear out your welcome." I knew that was more about not embarrassing him than anything else. For whatever reason, the abuse at that stage of my life went from physical and verbal to silence and indifference.

With Mom out of the picture, my brother with a driver's license, and Dad deciding to check out of my life in every manner possible, I officially had no one left. My grandmothers lived on the other side of town. While that wasn't really that far, someone would have to go to the trouble of driving me there or picking me up. There were nights I would ask Dad to take me to stay at Mammaw Millard's, and he would just tell me no. Then he would go to his room and close the door, leaving me alone. He didn't care if I went; he just didn't want to have to take me.

Sometimes I would be by myself in the house for several days. I had nowhere to go, and Stephen and Dad were moving on with their lives.

Strangely, I actually preferred, even missed, the physical and verbal abuse. Having him in my face, whipping me, at least showed some level of *caring* for me.

First, Mom abandoned me by leaving; then Dad did it with apathy. At least I never saw Mom. Seeing Dad all the time just constantly reminded me that I didn't matter.

Around this time, Dad started going on group dates with other single adults from our church, and he met a Christian woman named Jeri, whom he started dating when I was in seventh grade. Honestly, Jeri was a perfect match for Dad. Stephen and I watched him become the perfect gentleman when she was around, which was something we had never witnessed before. She brought out the good in him, maybe because he was actually happy with her. The relationship didn't change Dad's private behavior, but at least he was better with us when she was over at the house.

Both of them were reluctant to remarry, so they dated exclusively for many years. Stephen and I really liked Jeri, and she was good to us. She became like a second mom because she was around more than our real mom was. Jeri was one of the only adults to be a consistent bright spot in my life during my childhood.

The Safe House

To say I was lost in the transition between child and teenager was an understatement. I felt no one would ever find me, hidden there in plain sight among family and friends. I wondered if anyone would even want to.

But through all that noise in my life, whenever I heard a perfect union of melody and lyric in a song, something traveled from my ears to my heart and made me feel alive. When I felt the wind in my face as I rode my bike down a dirt road on a perfect spring day, I sensed a strange but comforting presence. And oddly, somehow everything I needed in order to create whatever was in my imagination was always in my room at just the right moment. All these amazing points of light told me there was something out there that granted dreams and brought better days. These solitary moments spoke to me, telling me there had to be *Someone* watching over me. I could just feel it.

This thought had carried over from when I had gone to church as a small child. In those days we went to the church where Mom's dad was the pastor. This was back when my parents were still together. My grandfather would be in the pulpit, my mom and her twin sister played the piano and organ, and Dad would be down front as an usher. So my entire family was on the sanctuary stage.

When the altar call began, I just wanted to be with all of them, so I would head down front. But as the family drama increased at home, I would hear the congregation singing "Just As I Am" or "I Have Decided to Follow Jesus," and I was often in tears, feeling so many confusing emotions. Every time I walked down the aisle during an invitation, people in the church would give me exactly what I was so desperately starved for—approval and attention. I bet I walked that aisle at least a hundred times to "get saved." My dad used to joke that my grandfather would probably look up and remark, "Uh oh, here comes Bart again." Dad would even tell Stephen to sit at the end of the aisle to keep me from going down front.

Our all-in-the-family church gatherings eventually ended,

though, when my grandfather left my Mammaw Lindsey for another woman and, of course, also left the ministry. As you may recall, Dad's dad had left Mammaw Millard and quickly remarried. I inherited a family history with an obviously poor track record for people keeping their commitments.

While I had gone to church all my life on Sunday mornings, I discovered what it truly meant to become a part of the body of Christ at First Baptist Church, Greenville, Texas, during the summer going into seventh grade, when I became a part of their youth group.

I'd been looking for a surrogate family—even if only for a few hours at a time—and a safe, secure place to belong. Once I realized such a home-away-from-home existed, I was all in. I mean it's *church*, right? They *have* to take you! So if the doors were open to the building, I figured out how to get there. If the church bus was running for any event, I was on it. Sometimes Dad would drop me off; other times I asked people to come by and pick me up. One way or another, I was at church when anything was going on. After school, I rode the bus and got off as close as possible, then walked to the church and hung out as long as I could until the last person to leave had to lock up.

Dad was uncomfortable with my newfound church obsession. Change, good or bad, was really hard for him. But I think in some ways he was relieved I was hanging out with the youth group rather than somewhere else. He did go to church but never to the degree that I did.

Because of his I-don't-care-anymore parenting approach, I never had to get permission to hang out at a friend's house, and there were plenty of times when Dad didn't know where I was. The only consent he required was anything related to church. Often, if I asked to go to a church event or on some sort of youth trip, he would say we couldn't afford it. So I became *that* kid for whom the church had to pay for everything. I took advantage of the scholarships donated by people to help students go on youth trips. On one hand, that created more rejection and alienation for me, but on the other, I wasn't going to miss out on anything my youth group did. I was grateful to get to go. It was worth it to me.

You know in TV shows and movies when the good guys have to find a way to hide someone from the bad guys, and they take the person to a safe house? Well, church became my safe house, a place where I could hide away for as many hours a week as I possibly could. I totally related to King David when he said, "A single day in your courts / is better than a thousand anywhere else! / I would rather be a gatekeeper in the house of my God / than live the good life in the homes of the wicked" (Psalm 84:10 NLT).

I was thirteen years old and about to start the seventh grade when I went to my first summer youth camp with FBC Greenville. That week I began to really understand the gospel for the first time. If I had to pick a single moment in my life when I feel I truly began a relationship with Jesus, it would have been during that week at camp.

Forgiveness, Family, and a Future

One evening at camp, the group was gathered around the bonfire, and Rusty, my youth pastor, talked about forgiveness. He told us to find a blank page in our journals and write down: "God, tonight, I choose to forgive . . ." He then told us to finish that sentence. To encourage us, he said something to the effect of, "Now, you may say to me, you don't know how hard it is for me to forgive this person. You don't know what this person has done to me. And I say I know it's hard, but if you have been forgiven by God, then He gives you the power to forgive others."

Rusty explained how God gives us His strength and grace to forgive so we can be set free from the bondage that anger and bitterness can create.

While this was fairly heavy stuff for my age, deep in my heart that message connected, and I knew that God was speaking to me. My dad had hurt me, but I needed to forgive him. I stared hard at the page as tears welled up in my eyes. But I just couldn't bring myself to write down his name.

There are times in life when God convicts us to forgive someone and, somehow, we manage to obey immediately. We express forgiveness, we feel it, and it is done. Then there are times when we harden our hearts to the Spirit, which Hebrews 3:15 warns us about. And so begins the long, slow process of recognizing, understanding, and dealing with the pain and hurt of what has happened to us.

As for me, in that moment I hardened my heart. It wasn't that I didn't trust God or want to forgive, but rather that I knew even if I did, my dad would still continue to hurt me. I guess you could say that, though I believed God, I just couldn't trust forgiveness. But this realization of the *need* to forgive began then and there. I just wasn't ready to let go of the pain that was still deeply affecting me every day.

From that summer on, I was definitely all-in with Jesus. I entered into what I jokingly refer to as my "super Christian" season of life. Anything I deemed to be Christian, I wanted to be involved in full force, and anything "of the world" I wanted nothing to do with. With balance, this can be a healthy decision for a young person, but I didn't yet fully understand what a relationship with Christ could do in my life. I was just working to be the perfect law-follower. My dad thought my obsession with all this spiritual stuff was kind of corny, but by this point, I was pressing on, no matter what.

The people at church, specifically the youth group, had become my new family. They didn't get to choose me, but I certainly chose them! Our youth pastor, Rusty, was like my surrogate Christian dad, even though he wasn't anywhere near old enough to actually be my parent. I didn't know what it meant to be affectionate or encouraged until I began to receive and accept these incredible gifts from those people in the body of Christ.

I embraced the truth that no matter what happened or what Dad did to me, God was ultimately in control. I became more vocal about my faith, less afraid to ask questions about the Bible, and more confident to state what I believed. What I discovered is that there's personal empowerment that comes with a relationship with Christ, and this, coupled with a newfound identity in Him, brings real healing to suffering people.

As I grew spiritually, I started slowly piecing together what my life could be. For the first time, I experienced hope for my future. I began to see that God had a purpose and a plan for *me*.

Three

HOLD FAST

To everyone who's hurting,
To those who've had enough,
To all the undeserving.
That should cover all of us.
Please do not let go.
I promise there is hope.
    —MercyMe, "Hold Fast,"
from *Coming Up to Breathe* (2006)*

Starting in my middle school years, next to Jesus and the church, I had five best friends: music, Mammaw Millard, Mammaw Lindsey, Kent, and Shannon. While all five had already been in my life for many years, there was something about the journey into my teen years, dealing with my dad, and my newfound faith that brought a deepening relationship with each of these blessings. These four

---

people's presence in my life, combined with my love of music, kept me grounded and growing even in the most difficult days.

The Magic of Music

For me, music has always been a pleasure, a protector, and my passion. The words my favorite artists sang gave me strength and courage and inspiration and motivation to keep going, to keep living, and to believe something better was around the corner. Music gave me hope when I felt hopeless. Love when I felt unloved. A reason to embrace life when I was dying inside. If a song moved me, then I felt I was alive for a reason. Later I came to the truth of knowing these blessings were all gifts from the Lord. Music was simply the conduit for them to reach my heart.

In my new faith, I completely immersed myself in Christian music. My Walkman and headphones became permanently attached to my body. (For you young ones, a Walkman was a portable cassette tape player. If you aren't sure what a cassette is, ask your favorite search engine.) These devices were spiritual and emotional lifelines for me.

Because of my obsession with contemporary Christian music (known to insiders as CCM), I know everything about my genre of choice. I'm a Christian music nerd, geek, and aficionado. I know way too much about the history, the artists, and the industry. In a strange way, I had a neighbor named Chris to thank for that.

Chris lived just down the street from us. He was a little older than me, closer to my brother's age, and was a strong Christian. And—key to the story—I thought this guy was the coolest ever. He was always super nice to me, which made him even cooler.

One day, Chris invited me over. His room had all these

incredible concert posters on the walls. I was instantly impressed and amazed. The one that most captured my attention was for U2's *The Unforgettable Fire*. Chris encouraged me to sit still, to fully focus on and truly listen to a song. To take in all the nuances of the melody and the lyrics—the lows, the mids, the highs—and the dynamics of the track. He inspired me to tune out everything else and zero in on what the artist was trying to say to *me*.

As Chris popped in U2's *Fire* cassette and hit the Play button, I sat mesmerized and soaked in every tune. As the last track started, Bono began to sing the ethereal, poignant song "MLK." (If you've never heard it, find it and listen!) When the track ended, I asked him to play it again. And again. I was mystified. I couldn't get enough. This haunting track had innocence. Passion. Simplicity. There was something special about it. Many nights, I would lie in bed and sing along with "MLK" over and over. In fact, still today I find myself sometimes lying down with one of my kids for a few minutes at bedtime singing that song.

Music had an effect on me like none other. It could make me forget about anything. If I knew Dad was going to discipline me, I would sing until he walked in. Then I would sing afterward. My catalog of cassettes was literally the soundtrack of my life. And now I was starting to connect the Spirit in me to that same spirit in music.

To this day, when I put on music, I have to *listen* and not just *hear* it. If I want to play you a song and you start talking, I'm the guy who will hit stop and start it over because I want your full attention on what is coming out of the speakers—not your mouth, mine, or anyone else's. The only other artist I've ever met who was as militant as me about that is Kirk Franklin. I know because once he was playing me a song, and I started talking. He hit stop, waited on me to finish, and then started the song over!

I have always gotten frustrated when people won't give a song the attention I think it deserves. In high school, after I started driving, I'd often pull over at a quiet spot on the way to drop my date off. She probably thought that was the cue to start kissing, but no. Instead, I'd turn up my latest musical infatuation on the car stereo, lay the seat back a bit, close my eyes, and tune in. If she would cooperate and listen the way *I* did, and not talk to me, but tune in *with* me—that was one way I knew if our relationship could go anywhere.

The first Christian music cassette I ever had was by Amy Grant, but the very first one that I saved up my own money to purchase was Petra's *More Power to Ya*. The band's name came from the Greek word meaning "stone" or "rock." They were the most popular Christian rock band for many years. While a lot of people in the church in that era debated the merging of Christian lyrics and rock music, for me it was a godsend to hear melodies like the ones I heard on the radio coupled with words I knew came from my Bible.

One particular day, Dad saw that I hadn't cleaned my room after he had told me to do it by the time he came home. I had also left out my jambox (a cassette player) with my beloved, hard-earned Petra tape still in it. He walked into my room and asked, "Is that your new tape in the player you left out?"

Scared, I nodded. He took the cassette out of the machine and snapped it in half.

The jambox was one of those super-large models with speakers that could be detached for better positioning. Let's just say that after Dad was done with it, you could put the speakers anywhere you wanted, but they would no longer work. He completely destroyed that machine. But the good news was that it wasn't long until I had another copy of *More Power to Ya*, and because Stephen was about to go away to college, he gave me his jambox. I just made sure from that point on I kept it all out of Dad's sight.

To be eligible to go on the church youth choir trips every summer, you had to sing a solo in a worship service. Because I really wanted to go that first summer I was involved with the youth group, I signed up to do my part to meet the requirements.

To be completely accurate, my very first solo in church was when I was five years old. My mom was a really great singer and played the piano, so she was my accompanist. Mom told me that after she started playing the intro, I stopped her to inform everyone that she was playing the song too fast. She said she was a bit surprised but then started over at a slower tempo. I sang "I'm a Millionaire," from a Bill Gaither kids album. (No, not about money, but riches in Christ.) I was told I did great for a preschooler. But at that age, the cute factor usually overcomes any talent deficits.

I hadn't sung in church since I was a little kid, so I was really scared about standing up there in front of everyone. I asked the music minister if I could sing with someone else, and he told me it was fine if I put together a duo or trio. So I recruited two friends who also wanted to go, and we sang a three-part harmony song that was popular at that time called "A Simple Prayer," adapted from the prayer of St. Francis. This experience helped me connect the music I loved to my passion for singing.

Back then, when a major Christian artist released a song to radio, the record label also produced an accompaniment track on cassette, a recording of the actual song without the lead vocal. Our church allowed us to use those to sing Sunday morning specials. They became the perfect way for me to perform in a professional manner during a service. With the real track, I could sing my favorite songs from my musical heroes and sound just like everyone I heard on the radio. Little did I, or anyone in my life, know the foundation that God was forming in my heart with Christian music.

My Two Mammaws

I was very close to both of my Mammaws, but Mammaw Millard, Dad's mom, was around us a whole lot more than Mammaw Lindsey, especially after Dad and Mom's divorce.

Cloris Leachman is a well-respected, iconic Academy Award–winning actress, so when we found out she was open to being in our film, she made sense for the role of my Mammaw Millard. But first you have to know that Mammaw Millard was quite a character. She was *really* funny. She wasn't trying to be; she just was. She was actually a lot like Dad, stoic and direct, but with an incredible sense of humor, though I didn't see that part of my dad until his last few years. She had a wit and wisdom I have never seen equaled in the many people I have met around the world. She was truly one of a kind. (And yes, I have more Mammaw Millard stories to share with you. Stay tuned.)

After my grandfather divorced her, my dad and his younger brother made it their mission to be sure all other men stayed out of Mammaw Millard's life. My dad and his brother sabotaged any efforts men made to try to get close to her—and they succeeded. She never remarried.

From my earliest memories, Mammaw Millard went everywhere with us. She and Dad were almost inseparable. She didn't live with us, but she was always around. She went on every weekend trip and vacation with us. Mom joked that Dad would probably have taken her on the honeymoon if Mom hadn't put her foot down.

In recent years, Mom also told me that the reason for this attached-at-the-hip closeness was because my dad felt so guilty. He knew the reason that his mother was alone for the rest of her life was due to his interference in any man trying to bring her happiness. His endearing loyalty was fierce because he felt he had literally ruined her life, and he was trying to make up for something a son can't possibly make up for.

This effect that Mammaw Millard had on Dad was why—even after his accident, no matter how many nurses it would take to control and calm him down—she could just walk in the room and he would submit to her. She always called my dad "Bub," so she just used his nickname and told him to calm down—and he would comply. That tiny woman could quiet that huge man with a single sentence.

Of course, this caused yet another strain on my parents' marriage. What wife wants her mother-in-law to be around all the time? I have to assume Dad was so strong and insistent that, as in so many other instances, Mom just gave in until she couldn't take anymore. As they say, everyone has their breaking point. Some are just quieter than others until they reach it.

My Mammaw Lindsey, Mom's mother, was an incredible, godly woman and a major part of my life. She prayed constantly, consumed the Bible, and watched Christian TV all the time. I am certain her countless hours of prayer for me have had much to do with God's grace and favor on my life.

After my parents divorced, and particularly when Mom moved away, both my Mammaws stepped in and mothered Stephen and me as best they could. In the face of my intense feelings of abandonment from my mom, coupled with Dad's abuse, my grandmothers filled a huge role in my life. They were the calm in my storm. Throughout my childhood, both Mammaws were such amazing friends.

My Best (Guy) Friend

A lot of my childhood friends were the kids of the parents in the adult singles' class at FBC Greenville. One of those friends was Kent, whose mom was in that Sunday school class with my dad. Although Kent was two years older than me, we became inseparable.

While in so many ways we were total opposites, we had the same interests and sense of humor. Kent is one of those guys who can become good at whatever he decides to do. He was great at sports, and I was decent. He was organized, and I wasn't. He always showed up with a plan, and I was always game to do it. While we were really mischievous and pulled pranks constantly around town, we never drank or got into any kind of serious trouble.

Kent and I really connected the week of my first youth camp experience. Our friendship was forged there, and we became very close confidants in each other's lives.

He was my only friend who had seen firsthand what my dad was capable of. After witnessing several incidents, Kent was terrified of him and didn't really want to hang out at my house. I didn't blame him. After all, he had a sweet single mom, and that kind of male behavior was foreign in their home. So we were always over at his house. Because his mom knew my dad from church, she would often call and tell him I was going to spend the night over there. He was always good with that. Dad liked Kent for some reason, and he didn't like that many people.

This arrangement worked for me. The truth was that Stephen and I didn't want any of our friends to be around all that much, in case Dad snapped. One time my brother and a friend were hanging out in his room, listening to music. Dad had told Stephen to take out the trash, but he hadn't. So Dad walked into the bedroom, with Stephen's buddy sitting there, and dumped out two full bags of garbage in his room—nasty food leftovers, empty containers with random liquids, everything. Stephen had to clean up the entire mess by himself, re-bag it, and take it out. He was humiliated, and that's when he adopted his own no-friends-over policy.

For a long time following that incident, Dad would threaten me when he told me to take out the trash, saying, "And if you don't take care of it, I'll come dump it in your room. If you don't believe me, just ask your brother." I never wanted to take the chance to find out for myself, so I always made sure I took care of the garbage when he asked.

The desire to stay away from my own home made going to my friends' houses that much more important to me. Kent was the only person in my life whom I told everything that happened with my dad. Somehow I was okay with him knowing, because he never judged or looked down on me or made a big deal of it.

Kent saw more than anyone else in those toughest years. Walking through that kind of fire with a buddy who knows your business and stands with you forms a unique, unbreakable bond.

Kent and I made up two-thirds of what we called the Three Musketeers. We hung out all the time, went to church together, and constantly had a blast. So now it's time to introduce you to the other third of that trio—and the sweetest and prettiest too.

My Best (Girl) Friend

Shannon Street's parents were my second-grade Sunday school teachers. That's how far back our relationship goes. In fact, they taught every second grader who came to First Baptist Greenville for twenty-two years. The story is told that one day after Sunday school, Shannon's mom said to her family, "That Millard boy—I feel sorry for the girl who marries him. He is wild!"

Shannon and I have gone to church together for as long as either one of us remembers. At that time, FBC had about three hundred members, so it was like a big family. There were no cliques, no hierarchy. Everyone got along and did life together.

Shannon's family was the opposite of mine. Her dad worked on federal government aircraft for Raytheon. His job was classified as top secret, so he could never talk about what he did from nine to five. They had a very conservative, very consistent home life. Their family ate dinner together every night at five thirty—on the dot. For me, they were a ready-made family. (Her parents are still happily married, by the way.)

Shannon is two years younger than me, so until she was in junior high, we weren't really on each other's radar that much. But the summer before my freshman year in high school, she came into the youth group as a seventh grader. At Vacation Bible School, she played piano for the younger kids, and I ran the slide projector for the words. I thought she was awesome, and I was crazy about her. She doesn't remember that, but it's true.

Shannon's Side of the Story

"Coming into the youth group that summer, I started noticing Bart and thought he was really kind and thoughtful. I was very reserved and quiet, so I was also drawn to his fun and adventurous personality. He always made people laugh and was a good leader. As crazy as it sounds to say now, I was thirteen that summer when I looked at him and thought to myself, That's the guy I'm going to marry."

Our youth group, led by our incredible youth pastor and dear friend Rusty, went to Glorieta Baptist Camp in New Mexico each year. The first day there, we were given journals and taught how to write down our prayers, sermon notes, spiritual thoughts, dreams, and goals. Starting that first summer, journaling became an important dynamic in my spiritual growth.

The first day, I noticed that Shannon was already writing and doodling in her journal. Then at some point it fell open. It was just lying there, staring up at me, with a message scrawled out in flowery prose as only a young girl can write: "I ♥ Bart Millard."

I stood there, trying to process what I had just seen and what this might mean. I thought, *So . . . this girl likes me too, huh? Well, she hearts me. Cool.*

Here Shannon and I were, interested in each other and away together for an entire week. One night during free time, we were walking around the camp, away from the rest of the group. We stopped under a very old, large canopied tree. After a few awkward moments, we shared our first kiss together. It was July 1988. (Bookmark that detail for later.)

We went steady that whole summer. Shannon, along with her parents, would come get me in their family car. I had my learner's permit, so I would chauffeur the family around town for the rest of the evening. Her mom would get in the back seat, Shannon would slide next to me in the middle of the front seat, and her dad served as my copilot in the shotgun spot. I was joyriding with my girl . . . and her parents. I even drove them on a couple of road trips that summer—one to Shannon's mom's hometown and another to a rodeo. Thanks to her folks, I was good at driving by the time I could get my actual license.

I spent a *lot* of time over at the Street family's home. Shannon and her parents must have thought it was odd that Dad never checked on me, but they never said anything. Her parents treated me like a son, and her mom and I picked on each other a lot. We had a similar sense of humor, and it was great to have that kind of close interaction and camaraderie with a mother, even if she wasn't my own.

On our "dates," Shannon's dad would drop us off to get pizza or at the movies. There wasn't a lot for kids to do in Greenville back then, so we just hung out a lot, together and with Kent, and talked for hours on the old landline phone when we weren't together. (Can you believe we ever used phones that were connected to cords?)

Shannon's Side of the Story

"Bart always hid what was going on at home with his dad. But everyone I knew was scared of Mr. Millard. One time at church, Bart put his arm around me during the service. His dad, who had been sitting somewhere behind us, saw what happened. He walked up after the service and, very seriously in a strong tone, told Bart to never do that again in church. That terrified me."

Later that same summer the youth choir went on a weeklong tour, singing at various churches. We all stayed with a family at a huge house on Lake Charles in Louisiana. The girls stayed inside, and the guys got to sleep on a large boat docked on the water behind the house. Shannon and I slipped away from everyone, and, standing there next to the moonlit water, we had our second kiss. (By now, you are probably wondering where all the church chaperones were on these trips, right? Ah, the innocence of those days.)

When summer was over and I started high school as a freshman, I thought it might not be cool to date a junior high girl, so I broke up with Shannon. Yet we managed to stay friends, because that was always the foundation of our relationship. The unwritten teenage social laws have always stated you are supposed to hate each other after breaking up, but we never did. It also helped that our youth group was so close-knit and that our youth pastor was a common bond between us, offering accountability and encouragement.

Shannon's Side of the Story

"After that first breakup, I always kept hope alive that things would work out with me and Bart. Plus, I noticed anytime we were around each other, he would show off and try to get my attention. This worked out great for me because I always wanted to be where he was. And, of course, we were always at church together."

By the time Shannon got to high school as a freshman, when I was a junior, our strong friendship had led us back into dating again. We hung out all the time, alone and also with Kent. No matter what was going on with Shannon and me in our relationship, the Three Musketeers managed to stay together.

But then, at the beginning of my senior year, the vicious lack-of-commitment cycle circled back around again. I decided I didn't want to date an underclassman, so I broke up with Shannon for the second time. (Do you ladies hate me yet? I admit I was a fickle jerk, okay?)

Shannon's Side of the Story

"We were driving in the car when he started telling me about wanting to be able to focus on his senior year and date other people. I was heartbroken, but I decided to play it off like I was strong and he wasn't getting to me this time. I said something like, 'Yeah, I've actually been thinking about the same thing.' When

Bart thought that I was okay with the breakup, he told me that he wanted to play a joke on my mom where he would go up to the door, tell her he broke up with me, and say that I was completely devastated. Still in shock but trying to be brave, I agreed to it. So when we pulled up to the house, Bart played off the joke, and then told my mom he was only kidding. He assured her everything was fine, she laughed it off, and then he left. After he drove away, I told Mom the truth and then fell apart. I was really mad at him, and then so was she. That time, I thought I was done and I never wanted anything like that to happen to me again. But I was so confused because I really thought Bart was the one."

Shannon was my first girlfriend. She set the standard that no one else could measure up to. She was everything to me, and her family was everything my family wasn't. She was so compassionate, with such a gentle spirit. She always cared about me when I felt no one else did, and she was always, always a great listener, which I so needed. I honestly have never known anyone quite like her. I guess that's exactly why I could never find another girl to rival her, even though I tried. Every girl paled in comparison. And nobody could ever make me laugh like she could. No one in my life ever cared about me the way Shannon did.

Because my home life made my middle school and high school years even more difficult than the typical teen struggles, I am so thankful for all the anchors—my two Mammaws, my youth group, my love of singing and music, Kent, and Shannon and her family—that God placed in my life. They all helped me hold fast to Him and find hope when I needed it the most. Little did I know I was about to need that support more than ever.

Four

NEW LEASE ON LIFE

Oh Lord have mercy on this weary soul,
Come and take me to the river and make me whole,
It's down with the old and up with the new,
The hard reset, my life, take two.

—MERCYME, "NEW LEASE ON LIFE,"
FROM *WELCOME TO THE NEW* (2014)*

One night when I was a freshman in high school, Dad was having dinner at his favorite diner in Greenville, the Royal Drive-in, when he started feeling ill. He had severe abdominal pain, and his speech became slurred. He wasn't making sense to the waitress, so she knew something was wrong and called for an ambulance.

The emergency room doctor ordered a round of tests to discern a diagnosis. When Dad's lab and blood work results came back, the

---

* Words and music by MercyMe, Soli Olds, David Garcia, and Ben Glover. Copyright © 2014 MercyMe Music (ASCAP), Wet As A Fish Music (ASCAP), Soul Glow Activator Music (BMI), D Soul Music, Universal Music - Brentwood Benson Publishing (ASCAP) and 9t One Songs, Ariose Music (ASCAP). All rights reserved. Used by permission.

doctor quickly saw he had very low blood sugar and diagnosed him with diabetes. Believing that was the sole source of the pain, the doctor released him with medications and instructions for managing his newly discovered disease. (It's important to note that while Dad was a tall man, by this point in his life he weighed well in excess of three hundred pounds.)

But his condition didn't get better. In fact, it started getting worse. Mammaw Millard and I noticed his skin was very yellow. Even his eyes looked yellow. Realizing he was severely jaundiced, he went back to the hospital. As the diabetes treatments appeared not to be working, the doctors feared that something else could be wrong, something much worse. They ran more extensive tests but were not satisfied with the findings. They informed us that they wanted to perform exploratory surgery. Reluctantly, Dad agreed.

About four hours into the surgery, a doctor came out and told us Dad had pancreatic cancer. We were in shock. He then said they were trying to find exactly where on his pancreas the cancer was located. If it was on one specific area of the organ, that would indicate he had only months to live. If it was in another spot, he could have several years left. When the doctor returned to the operating room, we sat in the waiting area praying that he didn't have the "bad" cancer but the "good" cancer.

After another four hours passed, the doctor told us they had found all the cancer on the side they had hoped for—that Dad should have a few more years to live. That was such a surreal moment. On one hand we were devastated that he had been diagnosed with terminal cancer, but on the other, we were grateful that we had longer than just a few months left with him. (As it turned out, there were many more times in this journey that we had to choose between the bad and the worse viewpoints.)

The day following the surgery, when Dad was fully awake and

alert, his doctor delivered the news of what they had found. He told Dad that he had pancreatic cancer, one of the most aggressive and brutal types. He went on to explain that the reason he had contracted diabetes and was jaundiced was because the cancer had spread to his liver. The doctor told Dad that, with proper care and treatment, he had, at best, seven to ten years to live. Of course, with cancer, there are no guarantees.

Isn't it interesting? We all understand we are going to die. None of us know how long we have. But as soon as a medical professional puts a number to our remaining days, it completely changes our perspectives of both death *and* life. That was certainly the case with my dad. When he received the cancer diagnosis, Dad was just forty-four years old. I was fifteen.

Mammaw Millard took the news very hard. Her ex-husband, my grandfather, was only in his early forties when he died of cancer. Even though they had been divorced for quite a while—not by her choice—she still loved him. Now she felt as though her nightmare was happening all over again, as her son had now received the same news in almost exactly the same year of his life.

That day, as soon as school was out, I went straight to the hospital. When we talked about the cancer, Dad didn't cry, even though they told me that he had after getting the news that morning. I saw and heard a noticeable change in his face and in his voice as he spoke. I saw what could only be described as a humility I had never seen him express.

Some might say I had every right to think Dad was receiving some kind of what-goes-around-comes-around, reap-what-you-sow cosmic justice. They might think I might even be relieved or somehow glad that this was happening to the man who had been such a monster to me in both the violence *and* the silence for so many years. And it's true that many days I had wished God would take this man out of my life because of the pain he had caused me. But now I was praying he might be saved—simply because he was my dad.

Reality and Repentance

All I could think about was that a doctor had handed my dad a death sentence. Regardless of the painful past, he had been my only available parent since the third grade. For better or for worse, he was still my father. He was this big, strong man's man, and I had believed nothing or no one could ever take him down—yet I had been told that something was going to do just that.

I looked at Dad lying in that hospital bed and thought about what must be running through his mind and heart. I felt horrible for him. Something new was happening inside me: the anger in my heart was moving aside and making room for compassion. Sympathy welled up in me, along with my tears.

Rusty, my youth pastor, came to the hospital. We found a quiet spot, and he sat with me while I let the dam break and all my emotions pour out. Any setting where I could open up with Rusty to talk one-on-one always created a safe place for me—one of only a few in my life.

I always knew my dad was physically strong, but in the days that followed, a different strength emerged in him. When Dad went to church before, it had been for social reasons: he wanted to be around other singles and have a group to spend time with. Now going to church was completely about the Lord, not the ladies. He also became gentler, more compassionate. The bottom line? Somehow, my dad was changing for the better.

It was as though whatever had happened to his mind years ago when he woke up after the truck accident had started to reverse when he woke up from the exploratory surgery. Years before, something had gone very wrong. Now—through a cancer diagnosis, of all things—something was finally going in the right direction for Dad . . . and for me.

An old saying goes, "The storms of life make you either better or bitter." I guess Dad decided he had had enough of *bitter* and wanted to try *better* this time. We have all heard about angry, resentful people who get bad news that sends them even deeper into a chasm of disillusionment and disgust with life. But Dad started climbing out of the pit he had been in for so many years. Or maybe Someone was lifting him out, and his heart was finally opening. Maybe he hit the proverbial bottom, looked up, and asked God for help.

For as long as I could remember, Dad's anger and pride had always gotten the best of him. He could never admit he was wrong. Now the anger began showing up less, the pride took a back seat to a new humility, and he began leaving room for others, including me, to have something to say.

I made a decision, even at that young age, that I had to stop being afraid of my dad. I knew I had to step outside of what had been and start to see him as a hurting and suffering human being. I had to care about him in a completely different way. I was forced to grow up really fast when Mom left us; now I was forced again to go to another level—mentally, emotionally, and spiritually.

I took on more of a caretaker role in looking out for Dad, and, miraculously, that cleared the way for him to be more involved in my life. Our new common enemy of cancer moved us toward each other, to stand back-to-back and battle the disease together instead of going toe-to-toe, with me constantly trying to defend myself.

Things were changing. When I checked on him at night to turn off his light, I would see his open Bible in his hands; he had fallen asleep reading it. We also started spending more time together.

Dad tried to exercise to improve his quality of life, so we walked on the local track, which gave us time to talk. We had always watched sports, especially football, on TV together; now we also watched comedies. We would laugh together, which we had *never* done before. I even got to the point of staying home with him instead of going out in the evenings.

For the first time in my life, we were *choosing* to be together.

The Pickup Project

Dad owned a 1963 Chevy pickup that had sat in the driveway for years. It was a hunter-green, short-bed, step-side model with a column-shift, three-on-the-tree transmission and the obligatory gun rack in the back window. (*Very* Texas.) For good reason, Dad didn't own a gun, so he kept an umbrella hanging across the arms on the rack.

When I was a kid, the truck was drivable but needed work. Dad didn't have the money to fix it up, so, eventually, the truck wouldn't run. Knowing we were on borrowed time, he wanted to get it back into operation while he was still physically able. He also saw it as an opportunity for us to have a project to do together. But I was still struggling with my conflicted feelings between the past and present, so I wasn't totally on board with the idea.

I think Dad wanted to make positive memories with me and maybe leave me with a cool classic truck to drive after he was gone. But I ruined that by not letting go of my pride.

The battle came to a head one day when we were standing at the truck and I was refusing to work on it with him. He got angry, picked up the spare tire, and tried to throw it as hard as he could across the driveway. For many years that feat would not have been hard at all for Dad, but with the cancer now sapping his strength, he was just too weak. As he dropped the tire, he lost his balance and fell down.

Frustrated, I walked over and easily picked up the tire with one hand. Dad just lay there, staring up at me, and in desperation said, "Go ahead, son, you know you've always wanted to do it. Take your shot. Here I am. Hit me with it." I paused, turned away, and put the tire back in the truck bed without saying a word.

Of course, while I had thought plenty of times about taking some kind of revenge, those days were long over. I wasn't about to physically hurt him now. But I realized my words and attitude were doing plenty of damage, just as his had done to me. I sensed a deep conviction that I had to find the strength to change how I felt.

I once heard a pastor say that when it comes to the sins of our fathers, we either repeat or repent. Dad was repenting, and I needed to make my choice too.

Dad had always told Stephen and me that if he could ever lose enough weight to meet his goal, he was going to trade in that old truck for a brand-new one. Unfortunately, the cancer eventually caused him to hit the goal, but Dad decided that, regardless of the reason, he was going to keep his word. So Dad decided that instead of us trying to repair the old one, he would replace the old classic clunker with a newer model.

The new truck also had a manual transmission, which I had not yet learned to drive. When Dad had to be in the hospital for several days, I got inside, pulled out onto the access road in front of our house, and ground those gears good until I figured out how to shift and drive it.

When he was released from the hospital, I surprised him by driving up in the new truck. Dad smiled the entire way home. He was pleased to see that I had taught myself how to drive a manual transmission.

The pickup trucks became a metaphor for our relationship. We had to give up the old, broken-down life for a new start to get where we needed to go together. And just as I learned to drive that truck, I was about to be challenged to learn a great deal more.

The Great Soupspoon Heist

Before his diagnosis, Dad would never have been playful in public, pulled any kind of prank, or done anything to make us laugh together. But one memory I have of how much Dad was changing stands out to me.

For some reason, he really liked the soupspoons from Royal Drive-in, his favorite eatery, and he could never find any like them in the local stores. The manager wouldn't sell him any, either, so he decided he was going to steal as many of them as he could each time he came to eat until he could get an entire set of his own.

He would ask the waitress, "Oh, by the way, can I get another soupspoon?" and while she was distracted, he would stick them, one by one, down into the shafts of his cowboy boots. By the time we were ready to leave, he had several spoons stuffed in them. Every step he took, Dad jingled as though he had on spurs or bells or something. He walked as softly as he could, shuffling out of the diner, but we always laughed for a long time when we got outside. By the time we'd eaten several meals there—Dad always ordering soup—he finally got his coveted, albeit stolen, set of diner soupspoons.

Eventually, Dad got worse and was mostly bedridden. Word had gotten around town about his decline, and one evening the owner of the Royal Drive-in came to the house. Dad hadn't been able to eat there in a while, so I thought, *Uh, oh. They heard about Dad stealing the spoons, and the jig is up. He's so busted.* Well, yes and no. The waitresses figured out what Dad was doing, and they thought it was funny to watch him sneak their soupspoons out in his boots. While I was sitting in the booth with Dad, trying to hide my laughter, the waitresses were evidently in the kitchen, laughing too. Like everyone else, they heard him jingling as he walked out the door. They started putting their scratched and bent spoons in a box labeled "For Bub," knowing they were going to get rid of them anyway. They thought, *Why not let Arthur get rid of the old spoons for us, since he obviously wants them so badly?*

Now, appreciating the regular customer Dad had been and knowing that soon he would no longer be well enough to come in, the owner brought him a brand-new set of those soupspoons, still in the box! Dad was a little embarrassed but very touched at the same time. That gift was a great example of what the community thought about Bub.

The False-Alarm Confessional

Following Dad's diagnosis when I was a freshman in high school, the doctor had described the kind of symptoms that would signal to us that the end was near. One night during the first year of his illness, I came home and found him lying on the bathroom floor, throwing up. He was wrapped in a blanket, shaking from severe chills. I hadn't been gone very long, so him being that ill so quickly scared me.

As soon as he saw me, he started to cry. "Bart," he said, "you know I love you. I've always loved you. I'm so sorry for not telling you. I wish I hadn't messed up with your mom. Please take care of Mammaw."

He thought that this was the beginning of the end, so he was telling me everything he wanted me to know, as fast as he could.

Dad continued sharing his heart while we waited for an ambulance. I just listened.

Just as he began to say all the things he would miss in Stephen's and my lives after he was gone, the oncoming sound of the sirens interrupted him. I had teared up when he talked about his absence, but the bright lights of the ambulance piercing through the windows as the paramedics pulled up to the house caused me to quickly dry my eyes.

After running a gamut of tests, the emergency room doctor announced, "Well, Arthur, these aren't symptoms from the cancer. You actually just have the flu."

It was a quiet ride home as we both replayed all that Dad had said that night. Thinking he was dying, he had shared with me what he thought were his last words. Believing that the end was close had made him become very honest about his life and where he was with those he loved. That night started him on the journey of opening up his heart.

After that, Dad made an effort to never miss any event I was involved in at school or church. But he also started going to things he never would have considered attending before, like parent meetings at church. He was sticking to the changes. Unless he was just too weak or sick from his symptoms or the chemo, he was there. Dad was committed.

After I got my driver's license, I started leaving the house more. Dating, hanging out with friends, and my social life took priority, as happens with most normal teenagers. But, of course, my home life had never been normal, and it certainly still wasn't.

Through the ups and downs of his disease, I kept seeing signs that God was most certainly at work in Dad. One night, when I came in to check on him after he had fallen asleep, his Bible was lying there, open as always. But this time I noticed he had been writing all kinds of notes in the margins. Throughout the entire Bible were countless scribbled observations and remarks.

I couldn't believe it. I didn't realize how much he was not just reading but *studying* the Scriptures. The apostle Paul speaks of how the Word of God brings about transformation of the mind. In that moment, I realized that God was literally changing Dad's mind.

Over time, we started to talk more and more the way a father and son are supposed to. Because his words were now seasoned with God's Word, I started getting a sense of responsibility as to who I needed to become spiritually, as a Christian. Dad instilled in me that my calling was bigger than just singing. My identity was not in my voice but in Christ. I was a child of God who sang, not a singer who happened to be a Christian. (It would take me years to truly grasp that one.) He knew my gift had a higher purpose.

Dad said he believed that even his illness was a part of God's plan, and he wanted it to be used for His glory. For a human with terminal cancer to make that statement, something deep and profound has to be going on in the heart and soul. Something *not of this world.*

A consistent theme threaded throughout Dad's constant advice was for me to do what he felt he hadn't done. His focus was for me to avoid becoming who Dad had been. But God was taking us both to a new destination—together.

Dad had a lot of false alarms as the cancer slowly consumed him. I'd find him unresponsive and call the ambulance once again. He'd go to the hospital, and I'd wonder if this might be it. But then he would bounce back, and sometimes he could even go back to work at the highway department. After the accident, he had gone into the surveying department, mapping out new locations and paths for road construction. By this point, Dad was overseeing a crew from an office and didn't always have to go out on-site.

Between work, home, and the hospital, Dad was in and out of the house, and so my life was a roller coaster during my high school years. When most of my friends were focused on having fun on the weekend and dreaming of the amazing adventures they would embark upon after graduation, I was dealing with the emotional battle of Dad's impending death and figuring out what I could do to help with the constant regimen of his treatment.

Divine Interruption I

Let me rewind a bit to introduce a new plot twist that happened during my sophomore year. An event lasting only a few seconds affected the rest of my high school days in a major way, and actually influenced the direction of the rest of my life.

After playing football for years in city leagues, I put everything I had into playing high school ball. That's what Dad had always wanted. His passion for the pigskin caused me to be consumed with it to try to please him. Even though things between us were beginning to go much better, old habits and human patterns don't die easily. As I took my position on the line of scrimmage, knowing a pass play had been called and I might get the ball, I remembered my dad's voice taunting me: "I don't go down when they hit me. But you, Bart, you go down too easy. That's your problem."

The maddening thing about verbal abuse is how the words you've heard replay in your head hundreds of times, even when the person is not around or has stopped saying those things to you. Like the tapes playing in my Walkman, Dad's criticisms and cut-downs were on repeat. But the difference was I never chose to push Play—instead, those hurtful words just randomly sounded off at the worst possible times. They were a lousy motivator, but they drove me to go all out and take risks to make a play. My end goal was not just pleasing but impressing Dad.

I had started out as a lineman, but I switched to tight end at the beginning of tenth grade and was just two months in at my new position. During a pre-game scrimmage, we were running plays—offense against defense—when a pass play was called. The center snapped the ball, and I fired off the line, running full speed. I ran my pattern, made my cut, and turned. There was the ball, thrown like a rocket by the quarterback, but it was high. I jumped straight up as far as possible to make sure I could make the catch.

While I hung in midair, two linebackers ran into me, one from each side, and hit helmet-to-helmet—with both my feet sandwiched in between. I felt the force of the collision, and then a horrible sting ran all the way up my body. The bones in *both* my ankles were immediately broken.

I fell to the ground in excruciating pain. I quickly realized whatever had happened was not going to be a shake-it-off-and-get-back-in-the-game thing. The coaches took one look at my feet and called an ambulance.

After the doctors reviewed the X-rays, they told me my ankles were shot. While they would heal, I could never risk more injury by playing football again. That is, if I wanted to be able to keep walking for the rest of my life.

So, with the sudden surprise of the elimination of sports from my schedule, I begrudgingly joined the school choir for my elective replacement. My singing voice hadn't changed when I hit puberty, and I could still hit the same high notes I had as a child. For an adult professional singer, that's awesome, but when you're a teenager having to sing around your peers, not so much. I had learned to save singing for church. Now that a wheelchair and then crutches were a part of my life, I found myself trying to anonymously, invisibly blend in with the choir kids. (Ewww!)

Isn't it interesting how some life-changing devastations are actually like the crossover switches on train tracks that take you in a totally new direction, often forcing you onto the path you were supposed to be on all along? God had certainly brought a divine interruption into my life, taking me out of sports and putting me into choir, but then my life took yet another unexpected twist.

Divine Interruption II

A friend of mine who wanted to audition for the school's show choir really wanted to sing the Paul McCartney and Stevie Wonder hit song "Ebony and Ivory," a duet requiring a male who had a high voice. So to help him out, I auditioned with him and sang Stevie's part. When Mrs. Fincher, the choir and show choir director, heard me sing by myself for the first time, she was completely surprised— *pleasantly* surprised. She pulled me aside and told me she was putting me in the show choir.

"Whoa! Wait! I was just helping my buddy out. I had no intention of this being my audition too. Uh-uh! No! I can't do this!" I protested. "What are you trying to do to me? I only got into choir in the first place to get my required credits. I'm not an overachiever trying to do extracurricular stuff."

She just glared at me and said, "You can and you will. And there will be no further discussion about it."

Not believing what was happening, I went at her again. "No,

no, no, you don't understand. I am a Millard. Millards play sports. Millards do not sing and act."

She was unshaken. "You have a gift, Bart. A gift. And in my class, you will be required to use it—or fail. It's your choice."

Running out of arguments, I tried another tactic: "I don't sing that Broadway stuff, and I certainly can't act!"

"I'll teach you."

I was growing desperate. I decided to flatter her. "Look, you are a nice person, a really good person. I like you. I respect you, but there is no way, *no way at all*, you will ever get me onto that stage."

She turned, looked over her glasses at me, and glared. She wasn't mean—just really serious, with that give-up-because-you-will-not-change-my-mind look. Actually, it was a lot like when one of my Mammaws would let me know when negotiations were officially over.

It was too late. Mrs. Fincher had heard me and made up her mind. I was, by golly, now in the show choir—like it or not.

I owe her a great debt for sticking to her guns to force me to overcome my fear and step out of my comfort zone to sing a solo on stage in front of a packed house of peers and parents. (Foreshadowing, you think?)

I guess you could also say that was the moment someone discovered something about me I didn't even know. It's one thing to believe in yourself, but when others around you start to join in and encourage you, it's a totally different dynamic.

Soloing in the Sanctuary

I was a latchkey kid, coming home to an empty house after school until Dad got home from work. So I often rode the bus to the stop closest to the church, went into the worship center, and sang along with my favorite Christian artists.

Church sanctuaries all over the United States sit empty most of the week. I took advantage of this at our church, using the worship center for my vocal studio for a couple of hours every weekday. I would sing and sing and sing. I had no idea at the time I was rehearsing for my career.

The church had a giant cassette tape deck, like my Walkman on steroids. I would fire up the soundboard and turn on the amps. One day, I saw a set of super-nice, over-the-ear headphones plugged into the tape deck and put them on. I reached into my bag and pulled out the latest and greatest cassette from Steven Curtis Chapman—a CCM legend—popped it in, and hit Play.

The next sound I heard through the phones was Steven's "His Strength Is Perfect," which was such a powerful message for me at that point in my life. I was immersed. Overwhelmed. The sound was incredible. The words went deep. As the verse began, I started to sing along . . . loudly.

You know how people can't hear how earsplittingly loud they're singing when they have headphones on? But I was in an empty auditorium—or so I thought.

Unbeknownst to me, Doug, our new music and youth pastor—who had no idea I could sing—had walked into the sanctuary. I was paying zero attention, lost as always in the music, still singing at the top of my lungs. He heard the music still blaring through the stage speakers, so he walked over and shut down the power to the system. But because I had on the headphones with the song still playing, I didn't realize that now all anyone could hear was my voice.

Doug heard me belt out, *His strength is perfect when our strength is gone. He'll carry us when we can't carry on. Raised in His power, the weak become strong. His strength is perfect.*† By this time, everyone knew about my dad's illness and how I was helping with his care, so the power of the message I was singing wasn't lost on him.

So now, the new worship pastor knew I could sing too. At school and at church, singing was becoming my thing, totally by "accident."

A Millard in a Musical?

Each year Mrs. Fincher and the drama teacher teamed up to produce a full-scale musical production, casting the roles according to acting and singing skills. True to her word, Mrs. Fincher announced they were putting me in as an extra in *Fiddler on the Roof.* While I wasn't thrilled with the idea, I figured I could just blend in and sing with the chorus. But after that musical's run was over, she threatened me with the lead in the offering of *Oklahoma!* planned for my junior year. I wasn't at all ready for that idea and just brushed her off. I didn't even audition for a role.

I forgot all about what she had told me—until the casting list was made public at school.

A friend walked by me and said, "Hey, Bart. Congratulations." Another passed me and said, "Way to go, Millard." I had absolutely no idea what they were talking about.

Just then Shannon came running around the corner, grabbed me, and said, "Congratulations!"

"What?" I asked.

"You haven't heard yet? I have to say, I'm a little jealous."

No one was more confused than I was. I asked again, "What

---

† Words and music by Steven Curtis Chapman and Jerry Salley. Copyright © 1988 Sparrow Song (BMI) Greg Nelson Music (BMI) Universal Music - Brentwood Benson Songs (BMI) Universal Music - Brentwood Benson Songs (SESAC) (adm. at Capitol CMGPublishing. com) All rights reserved. Used by permission.

are you talking about?" She told me to go look at the bulletin board where the director had posted the casting sheet for the musical.

We headed toward the board, and, sure enough, there at the top of the list, I saw my name as the male lead: "Bart Millard as Curly."

Shannon put her arm on my shoulder, grinned ear-to-ear, and asked, "So? How excited are you?"

At that moment, I was terrified. In complete and total disbelief. They had done it: my teachers had conspired together to cast me as a lead to sing—and to act—just as they had said they would the year before.

I'll never forget the moment I stepped out for the first time in full cowboy costume to sing "Oh, What a Beautiful Morning" from *Oklahoma!* While it felt strange, it was also oddly comforting. Dad, Mammaw Millard, Shannon, and Kent were in the audience, middle center. Dad was glad I had found something I could connect with since sports were taken away. He was proud of what I was accomplishing onstage.

Shannon said that when I started to belt the first song, Mammaw Millard leaned over to her and said, "Mercy me! That can't be his real voice!" Shannon assured her it was, but I think everyone was quite surprised that night. While they all knew I could sing, my acting put my performance on a totally different scale.

When my first song was over, I was completely caught off guard by the audience's response. It was kind of like the first time I had held Shannon's hand—it felt right and peaceful, like when you open a gift and realize it will be an important part of your life for a very long time.

My senior year, the teachers decided to put on *The Music Man.* They offered me the male lead again, but because I had a reputation as an unemployed comedian, I wanted to play Mayor George Shinn, the pompous but playful governing official of River City. I closed out my high school choir and acting career as the comic relief.

Mrs. Fincher was the first person to convince me that I had a gift that not only had to be opened but also needed to be shared. She was an amazing encouragement and inspiration to me. But professional singer wasn't a popular career choice in Greenville, Texas, so no one, at least at that point in my life, thought I would take my newly discovered talent past high school. Regardless, there was a new truth I had come to accept about myself, in spite of all the fears and flaws I'd been reminded of my entire life: I can sing.

Life Lessons from My Movie Dad

If you have been even a casual movie watcher over the years, chances are you've seen a film starring Dennis Quaid. Since his career began in the mid-1970s, he has appeared in every genre, from family films to sci-fis and rom-coms to westerns. Dennis played my dad in the film version of my story.

One of the first days of shooting, Dennis pulled me aside and said, "Bart, I really want to make you proud. I want to make your dad proud. I want to represent Arthur well. But I don't have him to talk to, so you're my guy. You need to tell me what I need to know to get this right."

In scene after scene, we talked about how he would interpret my dad to the camera. Often, as soon as the director said "Cut" after a difficult scene, Dennis would look straight over at me—to see if I was okay after watching something so emotionally draining and to see what I thought about his performance.

Watching Dennis portray my father was like working with a counselor, helping me process struggles and emotions from my past. In one particularly difficult scene, after J. Michael Finley (the actor who played me) walked out the door of the film set, I turned to watch Dennis. To my surprise, as the camera continued to roll, I began to see what Dad might have felt after I had left the room and he was alone.

Witnessing the struggle and regret on the actor's face brought me to tears. I had never thought, *How did Dad feel after something happened between us?* Seeing that was so hard but oddly healing at the same time. I began to consider what Dad might have gone through in those private moments, the grief and anguish he might have experienced from both feeling and inflicting so much pain. In a strange way, I felt compassion for my dad even while watching scenes depicting the abuse.

Being on the movie set was certainly a cathartic experience, and it brought up new emotions in me. They say that hurt people hurt people, and for the first time, that truth really connected. I felt sorry for my dad and what he had gone through.

Dennis also encouraged me that there were some things the movie could not depict, and I needed to hold them in my heart, just for me. He did an incredible job of portraying my father throughout the entire film, and his heart and sensitivity to me was so gracious. And, yes, I am certain that Dad would have been proud and honored by Dennis's performance.

Five

IN THE BLINK OF AN EYE

You put me here for a reason,
You have a mission for me,
You knew my name and You called it,
Long before I learned to breathe.
—MercyMe, "In the Blink of an Eye,"
from *Undone* (2004)*

While I was not certain about the exact moment Dad came to Christ, it was becoming very clear to me that he had definitely embraced the gospel. He wasn't very outspoken about his faith, but I saw the transformation in him in our home, behind closed doors. The man he was in private was now the same man he was in public. He was no longer the man I had grown up with. But just as no one really knew how bad my dad was before, now no one could really appreciate how godly he had become after giving his life to Christ.

One of the inspiring dynamics we see throughout the Gospels is how consistent and balanced Jesus was—being the same person to everyone He met. I saw that same quality become real in my dad.

Often I could hear him praying for my brother and me behind his closed bedroom door. Sometimes I would hear him weeping over the loss of my mom through their divorce. To go from anticipating a shouting match or a whipping to hearing the faint whispers of him praying for me was a personal trip from hell to heaven on earth.

While month by month there was consistently less of Dad and more of Jesus, the cancer caused his weight to drop from around three hundred fifty pounds down into the one hundreds. When Mom found out that Dad was sick, she started showing up a lot, trying to take care of the three of us. Stephen and I resented her because we felt that it was too little too late. But Dad and Mom started to talk a lot. Each expressed regret about their past and offered forgiveness to the other. I'm sure that time was hard but good for them both to have the opportunity to wipe away the anger and grief, to get out all that had been between them for all those years.

Later Mom told me that one night, they had started talking about their lives as our parents. They shared all the great qualities they saw in Stephen and me, and how, no matter how hard they worked to mess us up, we actually turned out to be fine young men. After all the years of dysfunction, it was nice to hear that they had such a positive and healthy discussion about how we turned out.

There was one complication to Mom's involvement in our lives: Jeri, Dad's longtime girlfriend, was at our house a lot, and we were obviously very close to her. In fact, Stephen and I agreed that Dad should have married her years before, though he said he did not want to "saddle her down" with his illness and become her "burden." The entire situation was strange to me, as so often both women were there, but Mom would be the one to wash Dad's hair and perform other intimate caretaking responsibilities. They all seemed to navigate it well and allow for each other's places, so I never said anything. But I also noticed Jeri often taking the high road and backing off or leaving to respect Mom. Jeri showed true love and grace—that's the kind of woman she was and why we all loved her.

Dad's relationship with Jeri had grown to be much like the one he had with Mammaw Millard. She, too, could handle Dad. Jeri was good for him, and he was always in a better mood and frame of mind when she was around. She loved the Lord, was always looking out for Stephen and me, and encouraged Dad constantly in his relationship with us.

The War Is Over

During my senior year, I started dating a girl Dad didn't like. (He always preferred Shannon to anyone else.) This young lady was a Christian, and Dad had no moral disagreement with her, but there were two glaring issues: first, Dad didn't agree with how I was isolating myself from my youth group and becoming completely focused on her; and second, he just didn't think she was right for me. (As a parent myself now, I get how important that latter discernment is.)

To be honest, I had become this girl's pet. I would do anything for her. I think Dad saw how I was acting and knew it wasn't good for me.

One day we got into an argument about her. We both got heated as the situation escalated. By now, I was essentially a full-grown man, and he was much smaller. Dad's anger got the best of him, and he snapped. He grabbed a dinner plate and, from behind, smashed it over my head. Pieces of china scattered all over the floor as my head started bleeding.

I was shocked. This kind of thing hadn't happened in so long. But his rage immediately sucked me right back into every childhood memory of hurt and rejection.

I screamed, "I hate you! I am done! I'm out of here, and I'm not coming back!" I grabbed my keys and stormed out, slamming the door behind me.

As I sped away, I had every intention of never returning. If *that* version of Dad was back, I wasn't sticking around to see it—living or dying. I was not returning to those old patterns ever again, now that I was old enough to do something about it. Finally, this time I *did* have a choice.

Just as I had always done when something bad happened between Dad and me, I went to Kent's house, even though he was away at college. And just as she had always done, his mom listened to me. After tending to my bleeding head, she called Dad to tell him I was there and not to worry. She recommended he give me some time to settle down.

I stayed at Kent's house for four or five days. Being with Kent's mother, one of my surrogate moms, was always comforting to me when these situations made me feel so insecure and alone.

As Dad and I cooled down, I thought about his battle with cancer and the limited time we had together. I finally swallowed my pride and came back home. We talked it out and apologized. But what was different this time was that we worked together toward a resolution.

We never had another issue after that. Not one. We lived in peace. I think we both knew there was no outside problem worth our time and energy. Dad was quickly losing his war with cancer. No disagreement was worth our relationship, especially now.

(So what about my relationship with the girl? Well, I should have listened to Dad. She ended up breaking my heart right before graduation. In fact, I decided to not even go to the senior party. I think I was the only one not there. Dad was right all along.)

Something about that plate-breaking incident and its aftermath opened yet another new chapter for Dad. From the moment I came back home, he treated me as an adult and gave me a lot of respect. And something about us working through what happened took away the remaining fears I had still been holding on to.

Confessions, Coaching, and Counsel

Dad had asked his doctor how he would die from this disease. Also a family friend, the doctor was a straight shooter. Typically, he said, the lungs fill up with fluid, and the patient slowly drowns.

From the get-go, Dad made it clear he did not want to die in a hospital. He was diagnosed with cancer when I was a freshman in high school and started chemo during my junior year. By the beginning of my senior year, as his symptoms got worse, we had moved out most of his furniture and set up a makeshift hospital room in his bedroom. After chemo treatments or emergency care, he would return home to his own private recovery room with all the equipment he needed.

During the last year, hospice nurses came to the house. The mother of one of my childhood best friends was a nurse, and Dad was comfortable around her, so she agreed to help during the day shift. His night shift nurse was a guy he became close friends with, and Dad was devastated when the man was killed in a car accident. Dad said he couldn't go through anything like that again, so he wanted to stop the nighttime care and just have our friend come during the day. In his emotional state, he couldn't take having to get to know and trust someone else.

During that transition, we also decided that Mammaw Millard would move in to help take care of us both. It would also be good for her and Dad to be together in this final season, because they had been so close for so long.

The nurse showed me how to give Dad his medications through his IV during the night. I'm sure this was against policy, but we were trying to accommodate his wishes to the best of our ability. One of the shots had to be given somewhere between midnight and four in the morning, and it took at least two hours to work through the IV, so Dad and I started having impromptu middle-of-the-night conversations.

In some ways, it was as though we had just met and were getting to know each other for the first time, at ages eighteen and forty-eight. He asked me questions about my life to get me to start talking. At first I didn't want to communicate much, but Dad was a captive audience and hung on my every word. He saw this time as a gift from God to make up for the lost years, but I wasn't ready to give in and get too close.

Early on in this arrangement, I had to put Dad's care first, over my own life, and this contributed to lingering feelings of resentment toward him. Because I was now essentially serving as the night-shift nurse, I either couldn't go out on Friday nights or had to be back home in time to administer the meds. But in classic Millard fashion, he kept chiseling away at me. Eventually, I would sit down and download my entire day with him and talk over any problems or frustrations I had.

As time went on, I saw the value of getting his wisdom and counsel. A new healing was taking place. I started looking forward to those late-night sessions. I even began to skip going out at all on weekends and would just stay home so we could hang out. I still have the journal where I wrote the words, "I had the first real conversation *ever* with my dad tonight."

Dad had immersed himself deeply in Scripture and learned so much in his walk with God, and he shared much of his newfound knowledge with me. He became my personal pastor, teaching me from an amazing mixture of life experience and biblical wisdom. All that I learned from him in those last eighteen months laid the foundation for my own life as a husband, father, and minister.

One night Dad and I were watching a video of one of our church musicals. He looked at the TV, smiled, and said, "Hey, there's Shannon. Boy, you better hang on to that girl. Don't you ever let her get away. You two were meant for each other."

I reminded him that we were no longer dating, but he continued: "Well, whatever you did, Bart—even if you don't know what you did—you're wrong. So get it right with her."

We both laughed, but I took his comment to heart as his approval of Shannon and his blessing of our relationship.

In the *I Can Only Imagine* movie, one of my absolute favorite scenes is when "Dad" looks at "Bart" and with a smile says, "Did I ever tell you how I met your mother?" "Bart" smiles and shakes his head. The scene fades as "Dad's" story begins. To hear my "dad" speak so fondly of my "mom," like a real married couple would do, was really special to me. That was such a brief but beautiful portrayal of the many intimate moments Dad and I shared together in those midnight meetings. He told me hundreds of details of his life, confiding in me as a best friend.

The Sewer Summer
(My First and Last "Real" Job)

I was grateful that Dad was able to attend my high school graduation, although he was very sick. As summer began, I needed a job so

I could make some money before I started college in the fall. After all, life still went on, and the bills had to be paid. So Dad contacted some friends and found out about an opening in the city water and sewer department. His likely motivation was to put me on the fast track to a city job so I could have a secure position in Greenville for the rest of my life. I interviewed and was hired.

Journalists love to ask musicians what jobs they worked prior to their careers taking off. So many well-known artists have crazy stories about what they did before music. Well, I'm no different. In fact, I'll put my work history outside of music up against anyone's story!

My duties at the city water and sewer department were simple. First, I was given the keys to a large tractor with a massive mower box underneath that you could raise and lower. I was supposed to cut the grass under and around all the city water towers and storage containers. That part wasn't too bad—just really hot outdoor work sitting almost on top of a large diesel engine.

But wait, there's more! Each week I had to go to the sewer plant and put on rubber wading boots, protective eye goggles, and a gas mask circa World War II, fire up a high-pressure water hose, and squirt all the . . . uh, human excrement . . . that was caked up like concrete inside the tank, the goal being to force it down the massive drain in the middle. The aforementioned doo-doo was piled about three feet high all the way across the huge circular container. Picture standing in a giant commode that has backed up due to a particularly large bowel movement (and not your own, by the way) and having to forcibly and manually flush it by applying a stream of water. (I'm so sorry. I'm just trying to accurately paint this picture for you.)

That job involved more gagging than you would ever think possible. In the blazing summer heat, my sweat pooled up in the gas mask, and I would be forced to remove the antique apparatus to wipe my face off to be able to see. But that would expose my nose to the stench and trigger my gag reflex, causing me to throw up. (I promise you I am not making this up!)

But that wasn't even the part of the job that ended my illustrious and short-lived career with the City of Greenville. One day I was mowing around a reservoir that had large, steep slopes surrounding it. I tried cutting the grass by driving around the sides at an angle, but it freaked me out because it felt as though the tractor was about to tip over on its side. So I decided to try another approach. I would point the tractor at the hill, drive straight up to the top with the mower down, pick the mower up, then let the tractor coast back down in neutral. (You're already saying "Uh-oh," aren't you?) The plan wasn't that bad except for one little glitch: at the base of the slope was a small, concave concrete ditch for rainwater runoff. Driving across that little trench going uphill was no issue for the tractor. But coming back down was another story.

When the back wheels hit the trench, everything stopped immediately. Now I was sitting at a critically steep angle with most of the weight of the tractor in the back. By instinct, I hit the accelerator and gunned the engine. The tractor didn't move, but the front wheels rose up off the ground. (In the eighties, we called that "poppin' a wheelie"—but it was never meant to be applied to farm equipment.)

I had obviously enacted some irreversible law of physics. There was no stopping the front end's backward arc.

I was strapped in by the seat belt and beginning to flip back. A thin metal awning on the tractor served as a sunshade, and I could hear the four support arms of the roof starting to buckle under the weight of the tractor. Then the truth registered, or an angel screamed in my ear, that once the weight of the tractor came all the way back, the roof was going to be crushed like a beer can on a drunken redneck's head—with me inside!

Just before the moment of impact, I unbuckled the seat belt and rolled out the side onto the ground. The tractor finally got hung up enough that it stopped before turning completely upside down, but let's just say that the entire contraption was no longer drivable. It hung in a precarious position on the side of that hill.

What did I do next? Well, I did what any irresponsible eighteen-year-old whose brain hasn't fully developed and who is scared to death but stinkin' mad all at the same time would do . . . I walked to my car, drove home, fixed a sandwich, and watched some TV.

When Dad realized I had come home early, he asked, "Hey, why aren't you at work?"

"I quit! I hate that job and I am not going back—ever! Ever!"

He never said another word.

I never heard anything from the city. Maybe Dad took care of it. I really don't know, but we never spoke of it again.

That was my one and only attempt at what Mammaw Millard would call a "real job." While I know this is a comical and crazy story, God's guiding hand just kept gently pushing and leading me toward His plan for my life. I was placed on this planet for a reason, a mission, and God was molding and shaping who I would be, bringing about His will for my life. Just as He is doing for you, my friend.

My father, age twelve, and his mother, Mawmaw Millard (1955).

Arthur Millard Jr., the All-American.

Dad at his biggest and scariest.

Dad (age thirty), me (three months), and my brother, Stephen (four) (1973).

Stephen (eleventh grade) and me (sixth grade).

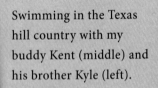

Swimming in the Texas hill country with my buddy Kent (middle) and his brother Kyle (left).

Dad, around ten months before he passed away. He went from 350-plus pounds down to 112 pounds at the time of his death.

All dressed up for show choir (eleventh grade).

Making my debut as Curly on the opening night of *Oklahoma!* my senior year.

Dad and me after a choir performance my senior year in April or May 1991—about six months before he died. This is the last photo I took with him.

Mom visiting twenty-year-old
me in Florida (1992). If there
was a piano in sight, my mom
played it and made me sing.

Mawmaw Millard.
"Mercy me! Get a real job!"

Shannon and me in our engagement
photo. Yep. This bad boy went in
the *Greenville Herald Banner*.

So excited to spend the
rest of our lives together.

MercyMe circa 1995. Left to right: Kendall Combes, Robby Shaffer, Jim Bryson, Mike Scheuchzer, me, and Trent Austin.

MercyMe on USO Tour in Bahrain (2011). Left to right: Dave Younkman, Scott Brickell, Dustin Reynolds, Jim Bryson, Barry Graul, me, Robby Shaffer, Mike Scheuchzer, and Nathan Cochran.

MercyMe at the Macy's Thanksgiving Day Parade (2015). Left to right: me, Robby, Mike, and Barry. (Nathan and his wife had just had a baby, so he was unable to be there.)

Recording vocals in the studio.

Me with Scott Brickell (left) and Jeff Moseley (right), two people integral to MercyMe's success.

Amy Grant and me at her induction into the Music City Walk of Fame. I was asked to speak during the ceremony. What an honor!

Three Barts on the set of the *I Can Only Imagine* movie: Brody Rose (young Bart), J. Michael Finley (Bart), and me.

With my movie twin, J. Michael Finley.

On the set of *I Can Only Imagine*.

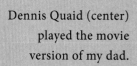

Dennis Quaid (center) played the movie version of my dad.

Mom and me.

The Millard family.
Back row: Sam, Gracie, me;
front row: Charlie, Miles,
Sophie, and Shannon.

MercyMe on Lifer
Tour (spring 2017).

Six

FINISH WHAT HE STARTED

No matter what you've done,
Grace comes like a flood,
There's hope to carry on,
He'll finish what He started.
—MercyMe, "Finish What He Started,"
from *Welcome to the New* (2014)*

During almost every late-night conversation, while the meds worked their way through his IV, Dad grew emotional and told me how sorry he was for the things he had done and how he had treated me. He expressed how much he wished he could fix what he had broken. But he also passed on hundreds of invaluable pieces of wisdom he thought I would need as I navigated my way through life, marriage, parenthood, and my career. To this day, I find myself

---

* Words and music by MercyMe, David Garcia, and Ben Glover. Copyright © 2014 MercyMe Music (ASCAP), Wet As A Fish Music (ASCAP), D Soul Music, Universal Music - Brentwood Benson Publishing (ASCAP) and 9t One Songs, Ariose Music (ASCAP). All rights reserved. Used by permission.

doing the very things he told me to do and constantly telling my own kids what he shared with me.

One of the biggest victories that came from those middle-of-the-night talks was that I learned for the first time to trust my dad. Honestly, that is a miracle, something I never thought I'd be able to say, much less experience. Who would ever have known, after the horrible impact he had on my childhood, that those soul-sharing moments could make such a positive difference in the rest of my life?

I had planned on going to Texas A&M University in the fall, and I attended orientation in early June. While I was there, Dad got really sick and had to go to the hospital, so I went home. That incident caused me to rethink moving so far away. I decided Baylor University in Waco would be a smarter choice. That way, if Dad took a turn for the worse, I could get home a little quicker. Kent was already at school there, and they had offered me a small scholarship.

But that August, as I was staying at Kent's place in the process of enrolling at Baylor, Dad ended up in the hospital yet again.

So after two tries of going away to school, I decided being even a few hours down the road was going to be too difficult. After all, every time he went to the hospital, we feared it could be the end. I moved back home just before the start of the fall semester and enrolled in East Texas State University, which was only about twenty minutes from Greenville. I could commute to class from the house each day.

Dad didn't want me to change my plans because of him, but I told him I knew I needed to be at home. I was all too aware that sooner rather than later I could go to college anywhere. For now, proximity to Dad was my priority.

Mirror Image

There were times when Dad was so sick that he would cry out for me to hold him, or he would ask me to change him in order to keep his dignity in front of the hospice nurse. Those were very hard moments for us both, but we bonded during them. He trusted and depended on me, and I did my best to unconditionally love him. Even when something was difficult or gross, I had to get over myself and help take care of him for his sake.

One particular day is forever burned into my memory. The hospice nurse needed to change the sheets on the hospital bed. There was not a comfortable place to move Dad, so I told her I would pick him up and hold him while she took care of it.

Dad was down to around 120 pounds. I easily scooped him up in my arms and stepped back to give the nurse plenty of room to do her work. As I planted my feet to stand, I caught something out of my peripheral vision and turned my head to look. What I saw was our reflection in a mirror.

There I was, staring myself in the face, holding Dad. He was limp, like a rag doll resting in my arms. For all those years, I had been so much smaller than him, living in fear of this large, gruff, angry man, feeling so insignificant in his shadow as he towered over me with intimidation and disgust. Now the tables were so horribly turned, and he was completely helpless. I was the strong one. But I had no anger, no bitterness, no vengeful thoughts—only sadness and grief that my new best friend would be leaving me all too soon.

In that moment, I knew it to be a privilege that God was allowing me to hold my father in the same way that my heavenly Father had carried me for all those many years. In fact, in these final days,

He was carrying us both, granting us the grace to see every hour we could spend together as a gift.

Go Chase Your Dream

So many incredible songs gave me strength and an outlet for all my emotions and feelings in those days. Not long before Dad took a final turn for the worse, I was scheduled to sing a solo in church on Sunday, as I often did. Dad was, of course, too sick to go. But when he couldn't be there, he always listened to the service on the radio. That Sunday I sang "He's All You Need" by Steve Camp. I still recall the lyrics: *When you're alone and your heart is torn, He is all you need. When you're confused and your soul is bruised, He is all you need. He's the rock of your soul, He's the anchor that holds through your desperate time. When your way is unsure, His love will endure, a peace you will find through all your years, the joy, the tears, He is all you need.*†

When I got home that afternoon after church, Dad called me into his room. He said, "Bart, you have an amazing voice, and I know you can do great things with it. I want you to know that I heard you on the radio that very first time you sang at church, and I was so proud of you."

What? I thought to myself, totally surprised. *He had listened?* It turns out that right after his exploratory surgery and his cancer diagnosis, he had tuned in to hear me sing at church, but he had never said a word about it. He went on to tell me that he had kept the radio on and listened to the pastor's message. Who would have

---

† Words and music by Steve Camp and Rob Fraizer. Copyright © 1984 Birdwing Music (ASCAP) Bud John Music (BMI) Universal Music - Brentwood Benson Publ. (ASCAP) (adm. at CapitolCMGPublishing.com). International copyright secured. All rights reserved. Used by permission.

ever thought that God would use me and my singing—something Dad had overlooked—to get through to him with the gospel?

I was speechless. But now knowing what had happened helped me better understand so much more.

As I sat down beside the bed, Dad went on: "God has a plan for you with your singing. You're really good, Bart. Listen, playing it safe is just not worth it. Whatever you're passionate about, you need to just go for it 110 percent. All in. Don't let anyone or anything stop you. Okay?" Through his tears, he told me to not let anything stand in the way of me pursuing my dreams.

Wow! What a turnaround from all those old messages he had preached to me about being realistic and taking no risks in my life.

Dad then talked about my finances. Although he hadn't made much money at the highway department, he had set up his retirement pension to be awarded to Stephen and me. He said we could take a lump sum right away, but he really wanted me to take the amount in monthly payments over the next ten years. This was going to be around six hundred dollars a month, which at that point in my life was an incredible amount of money. But then he explained to me the greater gift of why he wanted me to receive this blessing.

"I know for a long time I told you not to follow your dream," he said. "That's only because mine never came true. You're not me. You're not like me. You have a gift. A real gift. I want to take care of you, Bart. I want you to have the money so you can give your full attention to singing, so you can go chase your dream . . . and I want you to catch it. Don't you ever look back. You promise?"

I nodded. "I promise."

With a slight smile, in a sort of a half-joking yet oddly prophetic way, he added, "I don't know what will happen after those ten years, but I'm sure I will find a way to keep taking care of you." (Bookmark that line for later, okay?)

Not long after, Dad slipped into a coma. After a year and a half, our time together had come to an abrupt stop, forever, just when I had become dependent on those late-night conversations. I know they say you should talk to people who are in a coma because there is a good chance they can hear you, but our back-and-forth dialogue was now over.

His sudden absence created a huge void in my life. I wrote in my journal, "The dad I always wanted and have just gotten to know is about to leave me. How is that fair?"

But during those many months, in the still of the night while the rest of the world slept, the Lord had given me an example to follow—an example of who I wanted to be when I grew up. I wanted to be just like my dad in every way. Only God could have possibly orchestrated such an outcome.

A Bad Word and a Final Breath

Remember when I told you about my "super-Christian" season of life? One of the convictions I adopted during that time was that I never cussed. If I stubbed my toe or someone scared me really bad, I used euphemisms or made up my own nonsense words, but I never used any of the major cuss words. (I know the proper phrase is *curse words*, but, hey, I'm from Texas, remember? We say *cuss*.)

When Dad would hear me use one of those substitute words, he would always ask, "Did you just cuss, Bart?"

And I would respond with, "No, Dad, I didn't cuss. You know I don't cuss."

But he would press and push. "Are you sure? Because I think for sure I heard you say a cuss word. Yeah, I think you did cuss."

I would fire back, "No, I didn't! I wouldn't do that!"

So we had this ongoing game we played all the time about my "cussing." For many years, even after he became a Christian, this was my dad's go-to inside joke.

Stephen had gotten married my junior year of high school and moved an hour away. When the hospice nurses let us know that Dad's health had taken its final turn, Stephen and his wife, Darcy, came and stayed at the house. When he walked in the bedroom and saw Dad for the first time in a while, Stephen got visibly concerned. I had been with Dad every day and Stephen hadn't, so Dad's condition scared him. He motioned to talk to me outside the room.

"Bart, Dad looks really bad. He doesn't have much longer."

"What do you mean?" I asked. "No, he's fine. We have some time." I assured Stephen he didn't look that different to me.

But something about that exchange made me paranoid that Dad would die when I wasn't in the room. I worried he might slip away while I slept, and I tried to stay awake all night. Sometime in the wee hours, I sensed the Lord tell me I wasn't going to miss anything. Everything would be all right. Finally, I dozed off.

Early the next morning I woke up with a jolt. My heart reminded me about Dad, and, in a panic, I rushed into his room. My sister-in-law, Darcy, was there sitting beside his bed. His breathing was labored, and he was still unresponsive, as he had been for a while. But he was still alive.

Whew. Thank You, Lord, I thought.

But his feet were ice cold, which I thought was certainly not a good sign, so I went to get the hospice nurse. Just as I got past the bedroom door, Darcy suddenly called out to me, startled. Dad had reached out, his hand going for right where I had been standing.

I was so surprised. I hadn't seen Dad move in the past few weeks. I ran back in and grabbed his hand. Stephen came in the room and, from the opposite side of the bed, took his other hand.

Fluid was filling his lungs, just as the doctor years before had told him it would. His breathing became more shallow and faint, the breaths coming farther and farther apart. The hospice nurse counted the seconds between them and quietly, gently, told us that his time was getting close.

I watched the lack of movement in his chest. Finally, I was so anxious that I yelled out, "Damn it, breathe!"

Dad took a normal breath.

His eyes opened. He nodded faintly, gave me a slight grin, and closed his eyes.

And he was gone.

As I witnessed this surreal moment, I went from crying to laughing. In his final moment of life, Dad had finally gotten me to cuss. I hadn't had *any* communication with him in almost two months, and now, in his last breath, he got me!

He heard it. No mistaking it. He knew exactly what I had said. Game over. He won. Dad had nodded, smiled at me, and then left for heaven.

That moment forever marked the kind of relationship we had worked so hard for and forged together over the previous two years.

Dad went to be with Jesus on the morning of November 11, 1991, just three weeks before I turned nineteen.

The Empty Space and Amazing Grace

Dad died just after nine in the morning. We had to wait for Jeri and for Dad's brother, Uncle Mike, to get there, which allowed us to have a few moments together to say our final goodbyes. When the coroner took Dad's body out the front door, the hospice crew began taking all the medical gear out the back door. They wasted no time clearing the room; I assume their protocol is not to linger, out of respect for the family.

By noon, everyone was gone from Dad's bedroom, and I walked back in. I was not emotionally prepared for the life I had lived for the past two years to be completely gone in what seemed like a matter of minutes. That room had become holy to me, a sanctuary of healing and a place of grace. Now the room was empty. It was as if Dad had never been there. The finality knocked the breath out of me. I slumped down, melting to the floor.

I looked around the room in the deafening silence and stifling absence. One of the few items left was a framed picture of Dad and me. Without warning, an engulfing wave of grief swept over and enveloped me. I started crying, then weeping, then heaving, and couldn't stop.

My brother heard me, slipped in, and quietly closed the door so no one would disturb me. What felt like years of bottled-up tears flowed out of me for the next three hours. Especially for a guy, there are very few moments like this where you just cannot stop the emotion from taking over and pouring out.

The emptiness in that room matched the new hole in my heart.

I thought about all the late nights and the many words of healing and help Dad and I had shared. This room was the place God used to give me a real dad, a loving father, and an eternal example. This room was where, in my heart, God transformed the monster I hated into the man I wanted to become.

There was a time in my life when if Dad had died, I would have felt rescued. Honestly, I would have thought, *Good riddance.* But the change Jesus had brought in him over the past few years had also brought about a change in me. In fact, everything had changed.

When we open our hearts up to Christ, that is exactly what He does. He'll finish what He started.

The Cowboy Way

Several years ago a country hit had the line, *Everybody dies famous in a small town.* Well, as popular as Dad was, word had gotten out in Greenville about his death, and a lot of people had gathered at the house. Shannon, Kent, and several of my friends from the youth group were there. Uncle Mike, who was always funny, began telling stories about Dad. Mom had come, too, and Stephen and I decided that her entrance would be a good time for a break. We left to take a drive.

Here's another one of the Mammaw stories I promised you earlier.

Mammaw Millard always watched a lot of the classic western TV shows, such as *Gunsmoke*, *The Rifleman*, and *Bonanza*, and listened to old-school country and western music (back when the stars really rode horses and the boots and hats weren't just props to create an image). At the end of one particular TV show she watched called *Riders in the Sky*, the characters ended every episode by reminding kids to do the right thing. They closed with, "Remember, it may not be the right way, but it's the cowboy way!" Those influences showed up in Mammaw Millard's life in random ways.

When Mom saw Stephen and me walk out the door, she asked, "Why are they leaving? What's wrong with those guys? Why won't they show any emotion or let out their feelings?"

Mammaw Millard looked at her, then looked out the window and said, "Just leave them alone. They'll deal with it the way they need to. It may not be the right way . . . but it's the cowboy way."

Everyone must have thought, *What? The cowboy way? Bart and Stephen aren't cowboys! What is she thinking?* But that's the kind of quirky comment my grandmother would blurt out at precisely the perfect moment. It made sense to her, so it didn't matter who else got it. (Over the years, Mammaw's classic "cowboy way" line has been a long-running MercyMe inside joke. Now I've shared it with the world.)

Matters of Life and Death

To no one's surprise, Dad's funeral was packed. In the days after his death, a lot of people brought food and offered their condolences and support. But when the grief really sets in is when everyone leaves, when everyone goes back to their normal lives. Everyone except you.

What was real life supposed to look like now? I had no idea. After all, it was just Mammaw Millard and me—an eighteen-year-old and a seventy-six-year-old—living in the same quiet, lonely house.

I went to Dad's gravesite a lot. I also went through the normal ordeal of walking in the house, momentarily forgetting or denying his absence, and going to his room to check on him. I would walk over to a phone to try to call him. I would glance outside the house and think I saw him. And then I would remember he was gone.

When I went through Dad's personal belongings, I came upon a box of letters and cards that I quickly saw were connected to Mom. They had been written in the past year. It was clear from reading Mom's responses that Dad had apologized for everything. Mom also expressed deep regret for leaving him. It was obvious they had made peace with each other and wished they had worked harder to save their marriage. Dad actually stated in one card, "My biggest mistake in life was letting you go." Maybe deep down it was another reason why he had never remarried.

To get to read my parents' words of reconciliation was an interesting but welcome bit of closure. Dad clearly did all he could to make things right with Mom and ask for forgiveness. All those times he had read through the Bible brought practical steps he had taken to leave his business here on earth in the proper order to be above reproach in the sight of God and man.

In the following months, I realized how much harder Dad's death would have been for me if he had died suddenly. But near the end, I saw how much Dad was suffering and the pain he was in. I knew he wanted to be with the Lord. He was ready for heaven. That made my letting him go a little easier.

For so many years, Dad's anger and pride had gotten the best of him and ruled our home. He could never admit he was wrong. I really believe that had he not gotten cancer, he likely would have died a bitter old man.

I have heard many pastors over the years say that two of the most important words in Scripture are, "But God . . ." When He shows up, everything changes. After just five years of growing spiritually, Dad was a "man after God's own heart," the godliest man I knew.

He was ready to go. He was *so* ready. He wanted to stop the chemo and the suffering.

I learned from how he lived, but I also learned so much from watching him die. My dad had no doubts about where he was going. His faith was strong, and his belief was certain. We can talk big about death in church and in Christian circles, but when you are staring it in the face, that's a very different perspective. My dad embraced his death and trusted the Lord. He persevered and knew God was in control of both this life *and* the life to come.

No one else besides Mammaw Millard and me—the two people who had lived with Dad—had seen the change that Jesus had made in him. As we were driving away from the cemetery after the graveside service, Mammaw Millard looked at me with a sense of awe and wonder and said, "Bart, I can only imagine what Bub must be seeing right now."

Seven

BRING THE RAIN

And I know there'll be days,
When this life brings me pain,
But if that's what it takes to praise You, Jesus,
Bring the rain.
—MercyMe, "Bring the Rain,"
from *Coming Up to Breathe* (2006)[*]

When I was growing up, if someone decided to go into ministry, there was an assumption that he or she would serve through the few traditional positions available in the local church. Being involved in FBC Greenville's youth ministry had given me life and hope through tough times in my own journey, and I wanted the opportunity to pass that same love and care on to others. So I assumed my career path, coupled with my calling from God, would be college, seminary, and then a youth pastor position in a church. Even with Dad's encouragement and provision for my music, I decided to stay on the traditional ministry path.

Dad died in November, toward the end of the first semester of my freshman year. In the middle of my second semester, during spring break, Rusty called me. He had left Greenville during my junior year of high school to become the youth minister at Lakeside Baptist Church in Lakeland, Florida. He asked if I would sing at an event at their church, which I was glad to do.

During that visit, the two of us talked freely, as we always had. In those conversations, Rusty offered me a completely new direction to consider: move to Lakeland, work for him as his junior high minister, and enroll in the local university to continue my education. After such a difficult two years of caring for Dad, I was really ready for a change and desperately needed some new scenery. I accepted.

Rusty had been an integral part of my life, and working with him was a great honor and awesome opportunity for me. I went back home to finish out my second semester. In May, I packed up my few belongings, said goodbye to my roommate, Mammaw Millard, and moved to Florida to start writing a new chapter in my story. I arrived just in time to join Rusty's summer student ministry program.

I stayed in touch with Dad's girlfriend, Jeri, as much as possible. I would call to check on her and tell her what was going on in my life. It would have been so much easier if Dad had married her; then she would have been my stepmom even after he died. Unfortunately, she felt less and less like a second mom to me as time went on. She eventually married another man, and I was really happy for her. When she died, I went home to sing at her funeral.

It's funny how dysfunction can make blood relatives feel like anything but family. I guess it's like they say: you can't pick your family but you can pick your friends. Jeri had certainly been my friend for all those years, and I am grateful to have known her.

Planting Roots

I lived with Rusty until I got used to the area. Then I moved into an apartment by myself, enrolled in classes for my sophomore year, and started my ministry work. For the Wednesday night youth group services, Rusty had put together a worship band composed of high school students. I thought this was so cool; I had never seen a live band lead worship for a youth group, especially a band made up solely of students.

The guitar player was a junior named Mike Scheuchzer. We connected quickly, both personally and musically. With my love for singing and my desire to be in a band, it didn't take long before I was leading worship with them. So it was at that church, in a youth group worship band instigated by Rusty, that the nucleus of MercyMe was formed. Our roots were put down there. While over the years we have experimented musically, as all bands do, we seem to always return to this same kind of ministry—leading people in worship.

The youth group gathering was called The Attic, so we cleverly named the worship band The Attic Band. We worked up a strong set list of popular praise songs, and soon other churches in the area started asking us to play for special student events, Disciple Now weekends, retreats, and so on.

When I was in high school, the Gospel Music Association (GMA) had put on a student singing competition in Dallas. I sang Steven Curtis Chapman's "Waiting for Lightning." The judges told me that I sounded great—but they didn't like how I was dressed, and they thought I needed to lose some weight. (That was back before our politically correct days.) But the one important encouragement the judges gave that has stuck with me all these years was that everyone who had competed should start writing original songs to perform. They told us that all serious artists who maintain longevity in the music business write and sing their own songs. Music is not just about how well you can perform, they noted, but about what message you sing to the masses.

As Mike and I started playing music together, we began trying to follow that advice. As with all young writers, our first offerings were really rough. To quote Leon Russell, we "sung a lot of songs and made some bad rhymes." But at least we were starting to hone our craft. Before long, when we played at events, we would do ten popular worship songs that everyone knew and then throw in two of our originals.

Miracle on the Mountain

During my days in Florida, there was a well-respected student parachurch organization we often hosted called Awe Star Ministries. They traveled and put on weekend church events for youth groups, with a secondary goal of recruiting students to go on short-term international mission trips to give gospel presentations. They came through Lakeland regularly and put on their program at our church. They asked Rusty to come with them on the weekends to help with production of their events, so he would leave on Friday and come home Saturday nights in time to be at church on Sunday mornings.

After a while, Rusty began to burn out from working all week and doing the events all weekend, not to mention juggling the scheduling conflicts between the two jobs. He asked if I wanted to replace him at the Awe Star events. I respected the ministry and thought it would be a cool opportunity, so I accepted.

The Awe Star Ministries worship band was led by Jami Smith, a young lady who had gained a solid reputation as a respected worship leader in student ministry circles. One weekend she was scheduled to play at a different event, so Jami's backup singer replaced her. Early on in the first set, she forgot the words to a popular song and froze. Freaking out a bit, she nervously announced to the audience, "Does anyone here know the words to this song?"

Well, I had heard this set every weekend for quite a while. I had all the words memorized to every song and could sing them in the same key for a girl's vocal range that the band was used to performing in. (High voice, remember?)

So I left the soundboard, ran up onto the stage, and finished the song. In fact, I ended up finishing out that entire set with the band. It felt very natural, and I connected really well with the students.

Afterward, the Awe Star leadership asked to talk to me. Jami had been offered another touring job, and they wanted to know if I would take over fronting their band. Ready for just such an opportunity, I gratefully agreed. Isn't it amazing to look back and see the key moments when God orchestrates His will in our lives?

Now I was in a worship band with Mike in Florida during the week, and touring with Jim Bryson, who played keyboards in the ASM worship band, on the weekends. Another member was added to the MercyMe family tree.

In 1993, Jim and I played an Awe Star youth camp in Switzerland for kids of military members and missionaries. One day, as all three hundred students were gathered together outside, surrounded by the beauty and majesty of the Swiss Alps, we encouraged them to stand shoulder to shoulder in a circle. I jumped up onto a large rock and led us all in an *a cappella* worship song. I had never experienced anything like it—all those voices singing God's praises, echoing through that massive mountain range. To say it was incredible or amazing or awesome doesn't do it justice. That holy moment was the stuff of heaven. Indeed, a *literal* mountaintop moment!

As the students lifted up their voices heavenward, something happened deep inside me. Gently but powerfully, God spoke to my spirit that He wanted me to be a worship leader. This was about something bigger, wider, deeper, and more permanent than what I was already doing. I realized that I wasn't going to wait until after college or seminary as I had planned. The time was now!

It was my very own burning-bush moment. God had spoken.

Worshiping with those students in that setting made an eternal impact on me. I knew I had to be a part of leading songs of praise wherever God sent me. As I was standing on that physical rock in the Alps and on my spiritual rock in Christ, God connected my faith, my gift, and my calling for the rest of my life.

On the long flight back home, I replayed the Alps moment over and over in my heart. At one point I looked at Jim and said, "Hey, we have to do this. This is exactly what we're supposed to be doing. We need to start a band—full time."

After I got home from that trip, Mammaw Millard and I had a very honest conversation. I confessed to her that I hated college, which she was paying for. After hearing me out, she said she felt that if I did whatever I was passionate about, I would do well in life. She agreed to let me take a semester off to figure things out. She knew what Dad had told me about my music, and now she was placing that same belief in me. She knew it might not have been the "right" way, but it was the cowboy way.

You're Called *What*?

Mammaw Millard often called me in Florida, and soon she started to realize I was always home, available to talk. In her old-school estimation, she equated that with me not working.

One day she asked, "Bart, what exactly do you do all day?"

"Well, I've got my calendar cleared, because I think I'm going to start a band. All I need to do is come up with a name, and I'm good to go," I joked.

"Mercy me, Bart!" she shot back. "Why don't you get a real job?"

And that is how our band got its name. Really. No joke. Totally serious.

Some artists have slick managers, marketing people at record labels, or public relations folks to help them create a catchy, trendy, memorable band name. Who needs all that when you have a Mammaw?

Living Large at the Day Care

I would not be returning to college in the spring, and Mike had just graduated from high school in Lakeland, so I convinced him to move with me to Oklahoma City, where Jim lived. (Mike was eighteen, so we had to convince his parents too.) For the three of us to start a touring band, we figured it made the most sense to be centrally located in the United States. The middle of Florida is a long way from most places, but Oklahoma City is right in the middle of the map, with three major interstates running through it.

I worked for two years with Rusty at Lakeside before pulling up stakes and moving to Oklahoma. In 1994, three years after Dad died, Mike, Jim, and I started chasing the dream of a Christian group named MercyMe. As only God could orchestrate, our first official show took place at the same camp in Switzerland where the original vision had been cast.

Jim had a little recording studio set up at his parents' house, so when we came to town, Mike and I stayed in a camper in their driveway. Several months later, Jim told us he'd found a place where we could all live, with plenty of room for his recording gear. Intrigued, we went to go look at the property. We pulled up to the address, only to find out it was an abandoned day-care center. The windows were broken, and the inside was full of trash left behind by the various homeless people who had been living in it. The building had been vandalized repeatedly. It was in really bad shape, so it had been for sale for quite a while.

While we knew the building would need some work, we thought the layout was perfect for us. We called the owners in California, explained our situation, and asked if we could rent their building at a reduced rate in exchange for doing some upkeep on the place. I guess they figured some income was better than none, because they agreed. We cleaned it up, fixed the windows, made the classrooms into our bedrooms, configured one large play area into a living room, and put a recording studio in the other. It was the perfect band house.

Sometimes we invited a bunch of buddies over, opened up all the windows and doors, and played "Capture the Flag." Nowhere was out of bounds; you could go anywhere inside or outside the property—even on the roof. This game was especially fun in the wintertime when it was freezing and there was snow on the ground.

These were incredible, carefree days. Well, most of them. There were also the tough days, when the landlord would call about the rent being late or the phone company threatened to cut off our service if we didn't pay the bill. We didn't have the money, so we would call all over the area, begging youth ministers to let us come play at something, anything—even for a love offering—so we could make it another month. (Wouldn't our band adventures have made a great reality TV show?)

During this time, we met a bass player named Kendall Combes. Kendall played for other Christian artists and also did studio work. He was married, a little older than us, and more established, but the more we played together, the more we connected. Kendall agreed to become a full member of MercyMe as our bass player. Now we had everything—vocals, keys, guitar, and bass—covered by band members except drums, which we hired various musicians to play.

On the Home Front

On the morning of April 19, 1995, we woke at 9:02 a.m. to the sensation of the entire building shaking. Pictures we had hung in our rooms came crashing down. Twenty-five miles away from where we lived in Edmond, a rental truck filled with explosives had detonated in front of the Alfred P. Murrah Federal Building in Oklahoma City, and the nine-story structure was decimated in the terrorist attack. News reports said the blast was felt as far away as fifty-five miles. The rescue effort took two weeks as workers combed through the rubble. The death toll was 168 people—19 of those young children from the day-care center located on-site.

It was a sobering time to be a band traveling the country to spread the message and hope of Christ when the eyes of the world were suddenly on our own town. Because we were a local band, we were asked to play at some of the funerals and fund-raisers the community put on to help the families of the victims. We were humbled and grateful to serve in some small way at such a horrific time.

Not long after, we had to play an out-of-town event and needed to rent some additional production gear. The best way to transport everything to the location was to rent a box truck. On the way out of town, we stopped by the church where Jim's dad was on staff to borrow some microphone stands. We pulled up to the front of the church in the box truck, noticing that the parking lot was full of cars. As Jim jumped out of the cab, the church doors flew open, and men in suits came running out with guns drawn, yelling.

Unbeknownst to us, the church was holding a funeral for one of the ATF agents who had died in the bombing, and we had driven up to the church in the *exact type of Ryder rental truck* that the bomber had used. It never occurred to any of us what we were driving and how that might have affected people, especially so soon afterward and at an officer's funeral. Needless to say, we had some explaining to do. We felt horrible about the confusion and upset. We apologized profusely and explained the circumstances. Finally, we got the gear we needed and got back on the road.

Our days in Oklahoma brought a lot of great relationships into our lives, ones we still have to this day. We have even gone back several times to play benefits to help the victims of other disasters that have occurred in that great state.

Growing Pains

For traveling highways and back roads to gigs, we bought a gutted-out 1973 Silver Eagle tour bus to haul both people and gear. It wasn't much to look at, but the diesel dinosaur allowed us to have a place to sleep when we toured, since we couldn't afford hotel rooms. The entire bus interior was like a long hallway from front to back, lined with plywood. A family who owned a mattress company in Florida had given us a bunch of twin-size pillow-top mattresses, so we lined them two-by-two down the inside of the bus. We slept side by side and end to end. If the driver had to slam on the brakes in the middle of the night, everyone rolled from the back to the front. (It was actually kinda fun when that happened.) Fortunately, no one ever got hurt, but it was a crazy way to wake up for sure. We took turns driving the three-speed transmission behemoth in three-hour shifts, trying to ensure no one got too sleepy or fatigued behind the wheel.

With Mammaw Millard's blessing and Dad's six-hundred-dollar monthly provision, I agreed to work full-time for the band. I worked the phones, calling churches and ministries to book us. I acted as agent, manager, and road manager, doing anything I could do to keep us busy and get our name out there. The other guys got jobs to pay their bills when we were off the road.

We led worship as the opener at a youth event in Oklahoma in which Audio Adrenaline was the headliner. They were one of the biggest and best bands back in that era of CCM. Their number-one hits included what are now classics like "Big House" and "Get Down." Audio A's manager was Scott Brickell, but everyone just called him Brickell. He is a mountain of a man, a no-nonsense, straight-shooter kind of guy. (Trace Adkins was the perfect choice to play him in the film.)

As it happens, we almost didn't get to perform at that show at all. If we hadn't, who knows how our lives might be different today? Here's the story.

The woman sponsoring and promoting the event was a huge supporter of MercyMe, and she called Brickell and told him she had a local band for the opening slot. She went on and on about us, so he asked to hear some of our music. All we had at that point was a very poor cassette recording of some of our earliest songs. Regardless, she got it from us and sent it to Brickell.

He listened to the tape and called her back. Not one to mince words, he said, "I don't think this is going to work. I just don't think they are very good." She went on to tell him we were far better than the recording and that we were great with students.

"Will you take a few days to pray about it?" she asked. Brickell agreed.

The next week the woman called back. "Well, did you pray about MercyMe opening for Audio Adrenaline?"

"Yes, I did," Brickell answered.

"And?"

"Well," he said, "God didn't tell me anything different. . . . I still say no."

A few more days passed, and, determined to not give up, she called Brickell again. She explained how she really wanted us to play the event and hoped there would be more than just Audio A on the bill. Finally, reading between the lines, Brickell asked her, "Are you telling me that if I don't agree to *your* band opening for us, you might cancel *my* band?"

She responded, "Well, I don't want to have to say that."

The threat was clear, and Brickell gave in. But he insisted that we couldn't get onstage to set up or do a sound check until Audio A was completely finished and ready for the show, which might allow only thirty minutes for our setup and sound check. Thanks to some tough negotiations on our behalf, the deal was done.

We showed up at the agreed time on the afternoon of the event and moved our gear as close to the stage as we possibly could without interfering with anyone. The show started at seven, and the doors were supposed to open at six. Brickell finally cleared us to get on the stage at about 5:35 p.m. We rushed to get set up, even carrying Jim's huge Hammond B3 organ up the steps to the platform. We were still trying to do a sound check when the back doors flew open and the kids started running in to get their seats. We wrapped up and went backstage to get ready.

The event sponsor stood at the back of the venue during our set. Brickell said he had planned on walking up beside her, listening to about half of a song, telling her "I told you so," and then walking off. Well, he listened to half a song—and then the rest of the song and the rest of our set.

After the show, he came up to us and said, "Gentlemen, I was wrong about you. You are really good, and you're great with the crowd. Very nice job tonight. I know you aren't at the place to be able to afford a manager, but if there is ever anything I can help you with, just let me know."

At that event, we made a real connection with Audio A, particularly with Mark Stuart, their lead singer. They were all super-nice guys and very encouraging to us. The introductions we made that night would turn out to be yet another major God moment for MercyMe. Over time, we all became good friends, and Mark became our advocate in so many situations. He wanted to see us signed to a solid Christian label so that we could get our music out to as broad of an audience as possible.

As for Brickell, well, he probably regretted his offer, because I took him up on it in a major way. I called anytime I had a question. Amazingly, he always took my calls, when I'm sure all kinds of crazy young musicians just like me were trying to get through to him. Every time, he did his best to help us—at no charge. Let me tell you, that is not normal behavior for a music manager, Christian or not.

Brickell's office manager, Kim Davis, told me several years later that she always thought I worked for a charity organization because of the word *mercy* in our name. Well, we *were* starving musicians, so you might say she was right.

First Album and Last Drummer

Using our little studio in the day-care center, we cut our first independent record. We were blessed that Jim had attended Full Sail University, a comprehensive recording school in Florida, so he knew what he was doing. Our debut project was called *Pleased to Meet You*. (Get it? Clever, huh?)

Having our first actual project with our own original songs began to open doors for the band. This was back when not just anyone could make a record in their living room, so being in a band with a record to sell was a big deal and offered some real credibility. One of the local radio stations even played one of our songs. While we didn't sell that many records early on, the project helped us grow as artists, expanding our reach.

We hired the best studio drummer in the area, Trent Austin, to record with us. We hit it off with Trent and enjoyed working with him. Any time we would get a gig, we would ask if he could play with us. Because he was our first call, we considered him "our drummer." But he was in high demand and was often already booked, so during our stint in Oklahoma, we ended up using twenty-three different drummers. (Yes, really.) Some we hired once, others several times.

One of the guys that Trent had mentored and recommended was Robby Shaffer. He played for us several times and we really liked him, so we finally realized it was high time to commit to someone and stop the drummer drama. Of all the guys we had worked with, Robby played the best and fit the band the most. We asked him to officially join the band, and he gladly agreed. So not only did we have our first album release, but now the band lineup was complete. Robby may have been the twenty-fourth guy, but since that day, MercyMe has never had another drummer.

Music City Madness

We enjoyed our simple and innocent days living in the converted day-care center, but we knew we needed to grow as a band, and Oklahoma wasn't exactly a hotbed of musical opportunity. I was well versed in all things Christian music, so I knew that Nashville was the hub of the wheel from which everything in CCM spins. It was the home of record labels and managers and booking agencies and radio consultants and even tour bus companies. Music City, as they call it, was the one-stop shop. All the Audio A guys lived there. Plus, Brickell had been telling me if we ever wanted to give Nashville a go and play a showcase to try to get a record deal, he would help.

As we got serious about relocation, Kendall, our bass player, told us he would not be making the move with the band. He and his wife were settled and secure in Oklahoma. We understood, even though it was hard to hear. So, sans bass player, Jim, Mike, Robby, and I made the journey to the promised land of Middle Tennessee to see what God might do with our boots on the ground.

As a young band of starving artists with no money, we needed lots of space for cheap. Today, East Nashville has become, for the most part, the land of trendy coffeehouses and hipster hangouts. But this was in the mid-1990s, when the sounds of sirens and police helicopters were a nightly event in the area. We found a five-thousand-square-foot, three-story dilapidated house in a very bad neighborhood on the east side for a price we could afford. We assigned rooms, moved in, and set up the studio.

One night I came home and found Jim outside in the backyard with a .22 rifle pointed at the rear porch staircase.

"What in the world is going on?" I asked.

He said, "I figured out that the rat that's been getting into the kitchen is coming in at night through a hole in the back door."

About that time, just as Jim had predicted, the rat showed up and headed for his dinner reservation in our house. Jim fired the .22, pumping several rounds into the back stairs. He did eventually get the rat, but I was certain the police would be swarming our door any second.

Minutes went by. Then a half hour. We finally realized that random gunshots were so much a part of the nightly neighborhood sounds that no one even called the police.

All About That Bass

Soon it was time to hit the road. We had summer youth camps booked for two and a half months straight, and we had already been subbing in bass players for Kendall. Robby told us about a guy back in his hometown named Nathan Cochran. Nathan, who was dating Robby's sister, played bass and guitar and was a really nice guy. We asked him to join us at a camp, and he agreed.

It turned out to be a great week, and everyone loved Nathan. Jim was especially impressed after Nathan offered to jump in and help him work on the bus. (I think that counted just as much in Jim's mind as being a great bass player.) So in the summer of 1996, six months after Robby joined the band, Nathan came on board.

Little did we know that this lineup of MercyMe members would last almost twenty years.

When God Shows Up

The long-running five-step strategy in Music City to be signed by a major record label and "make it" in the music business is to play what is known as a "showcase."

1. Book a local venue with your band as the only performing act.
2. Stack the audience with your own rabid fans, encouraging them to convince anyone within a five-mile radius that you are the most incredible artist on the planet.
3. Invite every record label's A&R (Artists & Repertoire) person to come hear you.
4. Consider all offers, take the best one, and sign a major record deal.
5. Become rich and famous.

In reality, steps 4 and 5 rarely happen, but every young band or artist *believes* they will. And MercyMe was no exception.

Step 1: After attempting to book a few venues, we finally realized that our church home would be our best bet. All of us went to First Baptist in Smyrna, a southeastern suburb of Nashville. When we weren't on the road, we led worship for their youth group, so the church staff graciously agreed to let us play in the sanctuary.

Step 2: Working with the student pastor, we told the youth group about the showcase and asked them to come and invite *all* their friends to pack out the place, scream, stomp, yell, applaud, and sing along at the top of their lungs. Well, those kids did *not* disappoint. Pack it out, they did. And get into the songs in a major way, they also did. They covered this step of the Showcase Plan in major-league style.

Step 3: Brickell called in some favors and invited every Christian record label in town.

At this point in our career, we had ten solid original songs from our debut album, standard pop/rock CCM tunes about God and faith. At the showcase, we performed every song to the very best of our ability, but there was only one problem: when we finished the set, the students, whom we had told to go absolutely bonkers, just kept cheering for more. They stomped and clapped and shouted, "Encore!"

Why might this be a problem, you ask? Well, we didn't have another song ready to go! We hadn't considered that scenario. We had played literally every original song we had. But the kids just kept cheering for more.

I peered through the curtains at the record execs, who were waiting to see what we were going to do. But they weren't applauding. They weren't even moving. They were just watching the stage, like hawks waiting for the field mice to get desperate and run out into the open.

So we did the only thing we knew to do—we went back out and led worship, just as we did all the time with those very kids every Wednesday night.

It was incredible. It was like the Swiss Alps moment, but in the hills of Tennessee.

The final song we did was called "Behold the Lamb of God," a powerful and anointed anthem. When we got to the final chorus, we stopped playing and let everyone's voices take over. The crowd sounded like an army of angels, so we slowly backed off the mics. We quietly slipped offstage, and the crowd just kept going, *Behold the lamb of God, Who takes away our sin* . . . The kids in the audience were still singing with everything they had, pouring out their hearts to God.

You know true worship is taking place when no one notices the band has left. Offstage we were all in tears, listening, realizing this was the most important moment of the night. Forget steps 1 through 5. Forget the record execs. Forget the contract. Forget our band goals. This was why we do what we do. (In Jesus' name, amen.)

As the crowd stopped singing and people slowly began to leave, some of the record label folks found us. One said, "Your set was great, guys, but the really powerful moment where you connected with the crowd was that last song you did. The problem, though, is the whole worship thing. That's what Integrity Music does." (Integrity was one of the only record labels at the time solely producing praise music.)

"Sorry, but we just don't think we can market what you do, so we can't offer you anything." Down to the last A&R person, that's what they all told us.

At that moment, I had flashbacks of my dad telling me I wasn't good enough at football or would never be as good as he was at something. Rejection still sat at my front door waiting for an opportunity, way more than I would often admit. But this particular time, I was not just hurt. I was really angry.

I thought, *Market what we do? Are you kidding me? How did you miss out on what just happened? Can't you see there's something special to how people respond to these songs?* To say the guys and I were frustrated was a serious understatement. Disillusionment was thick in the air that night.

While our performance of our original songs was "great," we didn't have the right material for a deal, so the labels weren't interested in signing us. No one wanted to take a risk on the revelation and divine connection they had witnessed.

The whole idea of a Christian band leading worship and singing mostly "vertical songs" *to* God, versus songs *about* Him, was still a new concept. Just a few years later, the emergence of bands like Sonicflood and Delirious? along with the growing popularity of movements like Passion and Hillsong made worship music a widely accepted genre. In fact, for several years, the entire Christian music industry was almost solely producing worship songs.

I guess we were just a bit ahead of the curve.

Timing is everything, as they say. But God's purposes will always prevail.

A Clear Word and a Fresh Wind

We understood that the events of that night were certainly a word from God. It put an end to my desire to be signed by a record label. I was officially done—not with Christian music or the band, of course, but I marked "record deal" off the band's to-do list.

The next day we started talking about what to do next. We had a history of being nomadic, so leaving Nashville and moving again wasn't a big deal for us.

Around the same time, Mark Matlock, a popular author and speaker, had a major touring student conference based in Dallas, Texas, known as Planet Wisdom. He had called to ask us to start leading worship at their events, and we decided to accept his offer. It made sense for the band to be based in Texas and for me to go back home.

I called and asked to meet with Brickell. Because of all the help he had given us, especially setting up the showcase and pulling favors, I owed him an explanation for why we were leaving town. We set up a meeting at the food court of the Cool Springs Galleria Mall.

Brickell brought Mark Stuart, Audio Adrenaline's lead singer, with him. After they heard me out, both guys were adamant that we did not need to leave. They feared we might lose momentum or even quit after leaving Music City. Especially back in that day, there was a definite attitude that the only way you were going to make it in Christian music was to be based in Nashville and signed to a major label.

I assured them that MercyMe was going to continue, but trying to partner with the CCM industry was no longer our heart. We had given it our best shot. We knew without any doubt that God was calling us to focus on the worship music that we had now seen Him use time and time again. If the "market" wasn't here for what we were called to play, then we would do it from somewhere else.

Brickell and Mark understood. They gave us their blessings and, yet again, offered to keep helping us in any way they could. So we said our goodbyes.

Allow me to offer you a word of encouragement, regardless of what you do for a living, what stage of life you're in, or what your dreams and goals may be: During our time in Nashville, our sole focus was to be signed by a major Christian record label. At some point that year, 1996 to 1997, we had the attention of, and were in the running for a deal with, almost every major label. But each time, it would come down to us and another band for the one contract slot they had available. And every time, the offer was given to the other band. That scenario happened four or five times that year. But we did not quit. We heard from God and chose to obey His calling and direction.

Today, by God's grace, we are still at it: still making music, still making a living, still touring, still getting radio airplay, and still selling well. We all face really hard seasons when it seems as if the entire world is against us, when we think we just cannot win. But when we keep standing strong, following the Lord, and obeying His calling, He will see us through and keep us on His path. We're living proof of that truth.

God made it very clear to each of us that MercyMe's mission in this new season was to help feed the growing hunger in the body of Christ for this fresh wave of worship music. As our song says, *I know there'll be days when this life brings me pain, but if that's what it takes to praise You, Jesus, bring the rain.*

Eight

BEAUTIFUL

You're beautiful,
You are treasured,
You are sacred,
You are His,
You're beautiful.
—MercyMe, "Beautiful,"
from *The Worship Project* (1999)*

No matter what was going on in our lives, Shannon and I always stayed in touch. We never went too long without one of us reaching out to the other. No matter where I was in the country or how busy she was at college, we always found time to talk regularly on the phone. She would tell me about her relationships, and I would tell her about mine. Typically, we would tell each other that whomever the other one was dating at the time wasn't right and that it was

---

* Words and music by Nathan Cochran. Copyright © 1999 Simpleville Music (ASCAP). All rights reserved. Used by permission.

never going to work. It was our regular thing to discourage each other about anyone we were dating.

While Shannon was attending Stephen F. Austin University in Nacogdoches, Texas, about 150 miles southeast of Greenville, she dated a guy she ended up being in a relationship with for six years. (*Six years!*) She grew up in a stable home with parents whose marriage was solid, so when she committed, she *committed*. I dated a lot of different girls over the same time period, and the relationships lasted anywhere from just one or two dates to several months. But as girls came in and out of my life, Shannon remained the one common female thread throughout.

When I was in Florida, working with Rusty, she called to say her family was coming to Disney World for vacation, and they wanted to see me. I invited them to stay in my apartment so they could save money on the trip. To the outside world, we seemed to have a super-close brother-sister relationship, but in reality it was much more of a best-friend scenario. Built on this strong foundation, our friendship always had potential to turn into something more. No matter where I lived or whom we dated, Shannon was a constant source of stability throughout my crazy, nomadic life.

Love Is a Battlefield

In December 1996, just before the band moved back to Texas, Shannon called me in Nashville. She and a friend had just finished their college finals and were thinking about making a road trip to Music City. Because the band was living in the previously mentioned East Nashville house, complete with bullet holes in the back porch stairs, I told her there was plenty of room; they were welcome to stay with us, and we would give them their own bedroom and bathroom for privacy. (I didn't mention the rat problem.)

What I had failed to understand was that part of Shannon's goal in the visit was to hang out with me. I thought she wanted to sightsee with her friend and have a free place to stay. After all, she was dating the "six-year guy," and I was seeing a girl in Nashville.

I took her to dinner one night and we caught up, but I was busy the rest of the time. I didn't know she was upset that I hadn't made much time for her.

Shannon's Side of the Story

"I got to Nashville and Bart was dating a girl there. But we've always been able to hang out, no matter whether either of us was dating. I was thinking we were going to spend some time together, but I quickly saw that was not going to happen. We did have dinner one night, but then the next night, he was sitting out in the driveway in the car talking with his girl. I'm inside, peeking out the curtains at them. I finally got mad, and we ended up leaving early. In fact, we left one evening and drove all night so as to not stay at Bart's any longer. But the anger didn't last—and neither did our other relationships. Even though I dated other guys, they all knew they were second to Bart and I cared more for him. When he came around, I always made time."

Christian bands typically don't travel around the holidays, unless they have released a Christmas album or are going on a holiday tour. During December, most churches focus on their Sunday school gatherings, Advent programs, and nativity pageants. So

I headed home for Christmas just a few days after Shannon had made her abrupt exit from my house in Nashville.

On Sunday morning, I sat down beside her in the church pew and asked, "So why did you just leave town so quickly without even saying goodbye?"

She grinned and answered, "Because you were being such a jerk."

We both laughed. I told her I was sorry, and we were quickly back to our old selves again.

Save the Best for Last

Remember Kent, our third Musketeer? Well, Kent was getting married at the beginning of the new year, so Shannon and I were looking forward to his wedding. Honestly, it almost overshadowed Christmas that year. We both planned on being part of all the festivities. (I mean, how great could Kent's wedding be if all Three Musketeers weren't there to celebrate?)

Because a lot of our friends had left town after New Year's Day, Shannon and I ended up hanging out the entire time the week before the wedding. The first night, she talked to me for hours about her longtime boyfriend. As was typical, I just kept telling her that she needed to break up with him sooner than later.

Don't get me wrong—I listened and heard her out as she processed the relationship. But my advice *never* changed.

I had told many of my friends, "If I could find someone like Shannon, my problems would be solved. I end up comparing every girl I date to her." That night I *almost* told her what I had been telling everyone else, but I caught myself just before it slipped out of my mouth.

Then the truth finally took root. It had been standing right in front of me the entire time, for all those years, as I went through girl after girl.

Vanessa Williams had a hit song years ago, "Save the Best for Last," about finally realizing the right one had been in front of you all along. I *had* been saving the best for last, and thank God she was still available.

Through our conversations early that week, we each realized we were never going to marry the people we were dating. Without knowing what the other was doing, Shannon and I called off our other relationships. I wasn't 100 percent sure everything was going to work out with Shannon, but I knew in my heart that no girl deserved to be compared to another the way I was doing. I knew it wasn't fair to her and not right for either of us. I was glad to finally get the shot of courage to say no, no matter what might happen in any other relationship.

Late that week, we had a heartfelt, honest talk about the elephant in the room. We asked each other what in the world we had been doing with these other people when we were obviously supposed to be together. And then came the bombshell—we each realized the other had broken off the current relationship.

I was looking for another Shannon and not finding her. She was looking for another Bart and not finding him. So here we were, finally facing the truth together.

God seemed to be making it quite clear what He had in store for us. We had finally confessed our feelings to each other, and then that week culminated in us going together to our best friend's wedding. How much more encouragement did we need? Now we just had to give it all to the Lord for His timing. We prayed about what these changes meant for our future and asked God to reveal His will to us.

Shannon's Side of the Story

"That Christmas I was a senior in college. I knew in my heart the guy I was dating was not right for me. He wasn't seeking the Lord. I even asked him to quote John 3:16, and he didn't know it. I wasn't trying to judge him; I just realized he was not going to be able to lead me spiritually in the way God wanted—and I wanted. So, while I felt really bad about handling it this way, I broke up with him on the phone over Christmas break. I had made up my mind and didn't want to have to dread going back to school, knowing I would be ending it right at the start of the spring semester. I wanted us both to have the space between semesters and go back in January with a fresh start.

"Bart had come home for Christmas, too, and we started hanging out again every day before the wedding. He ended up breaking up with his girlfriend around the same time I did with my boyfriend. We spent a lot of time with each other that week. Then, at the wedding, something happened. After that, we started dating again. The Lord gave me obvious signs of confirmation. There was just peace.

"Bart and I connected so easily and naturally. It wasn't work at all—just a new dimension to our long-term friendship. Our relationship really felt like home."

You Know Me

One day not long after we had started praying for God's guidance, I read Psalm 139:

> You have searched me, Lord,
> and you know me.

You know when I sit and when I rise;

> you perceive my thoughts from afar.

You discern my going out and my lying down;

> you are familiar with all my ways.

Before a word is on my tongue

> you, LORD, know it completely. (vv. 1–4)

I thought of how Shannon had been so present throughout my life, how well she knew me. *Really* knew me. God knew everything about me, and I felt His intention was for Shannon and me to be together. There was always a sacredness and purity about my relationship with her, even in the midst of all the craziness of my life.

I called Shannon and told her I needed to see her. She told me there was something she wanted to share with me too. When we got together that evening, I—Southern gentleman that I am—insisted, "You go first."

Shannon's Side of the Story

"Rebecca St. James, a popular Christian singer at the time, had a song called 'Psalm 139.' The words from the passage really moved me, and I wanted to play the song for Bart. But he said he had something to read to me. I could see he had his Bible opened to Psalms as I played him the song and told him the story. Then he showed me what he was going to read me. God had brought us to the same scripture! I thought, I've known since I was thirteen, and this is it."

When Shannon was done, I was in shock. I told her I had the same experience reading that exact Scripture passage.

The Holy Spirit used His Word to tell us He created us for each other from the very beginning and then orchestrated our individual circumstances so we could now be together. Talk about a handwritten message from God Himself!

But You Surpass Them All

When someone asks me to describe Shannon, the first words that come to mind are *innocent, forgiving, kind, encouraging, intelligent,* and *just plain awesome.* She has always been the sweetest person I have ever known. She has no hidden agenda and no ulterior motives behind her love and care for people.

Everything about Shannon was better than me. People jokingly say about their significant others, "She's my better half," but I can tell you that, for me, it is completely and absolutely true.

I had always found something about every girl I dated that would drive me crazy, some personality trait or quirk that I couldn't stand. That wasn't true with Shannon.

There were so many times when the other girls would say or do something and I would think, *Shannon would never say that* or *Shannon would never do that.*

I could find flaws in everyone in my life—except Shannon. Of course I know she *does* have flaws, but I was so in love with her that I did not care. I wasn't focused on negatives but rather on who she was—and who I was when I was with her.

Shannon makes me a better Bart. No question.

Return Engagement

By January 1997, we had realized what God already knew: we were meant to be together. Two months later, in March, the band was booked to play at a student event in Glorieta, New Mexico, at the same camp where Shannon and I first started to hang out. She was going to be on her spring break, so she asked about going with us. Of course, I agreed. Then I realized I would be able to take her back to the same tree where we had our first kiss. That gave me an idea.

Just as I had on that summer night all those years ago, I asked her to take a walk with me, and I led her to our tree. I stopped under the overhanging branches, got down on one knee, took out the engagement ring, and asked her to marry me.

She said yes! (You weren't surprised, were you?)

She was graduating from college in May, and we wanted to plan the wedding to happen as soon as possible after she got her diploma. Shannon's parents had gotten married on Saturday, November 8—and in 1997, the date was also on a Saturday. Perfect! We thought it was such a great legacy for us to follow in the footsteps of her mom and dad.

On the Road Again

When the band had moved from Nashville back to the Dallas area, I had moved to Arlington, a part of the Dallas–Fort Worth metroplex. After our wedding and honeymoon, Shannon and I lived there to be centrally located but still near our families in Greenville, about seventy-five miles away. Although Shannon had her degree in psychology and counseling, for three months she worked a full-time office job at the University of Texas at Arlington so we could make ends meet. I was on the road constantly, and we didn't see each other nearly enough, especially for newlyweds.

One day when we were talking about the frustration of being apart so much, I reached my limit and blurted, "Just quit and come on the road with me."

Shannon's mouth dropped open and all she could manage was, "What?"

Always the solid, conservative, responsible one in this union, she started giving me ninety-nine reasons why that wouldn't work, with most of them having to do with money.

But I insisted. "The money will come . . . somehow. We'll trust God for what we need."

Mustering up her faith, Shannon put in her notice at the university, and we hit the road together.

Shannon's Side of the Story

"Quitting my job and going on the road with Bart was a decision that ran opposite of the way I was raised. But we did it for our marriage.

"I started traveling with four guys and my husband in a stripped-down bus with no air conditioning and no heat. And we traveled all over the country, in all four seasons. Some mornings when I woke up on the twin mattresses where we all slept, I would find myself nose-to-nose with Jim or Mike instead of Bart. When I say we were all close, I mean literally.

"But with all the inconveniences, especially for a girl, I thought this life was awesome. I loved it! Growing up, my family wasn't able to go on very many vacations or trips, so this was heaven to me. I was getting to see the world, and I was absolutely fine hanging out with guys all the time. There was never any drama. There was constant fun. We were always laughing. I never, ever complained."

In my humble opinion, while Shannon has always been an optimist, I do remember *some* drama and a *little* complaining from time to time during those years on the road. Here are a couple of memorable stories from those days.

One winter we were given a small propane heater to use on the bus. Early one morning we stopped to eat breakfast at a diner. Shannon was still asleep, and we didn't want to wake her, so we left her on the bus alone. (You're saying "Uh, oh" again, aren't you?) On the way out the door, we decided to start up the heater to keep her warm.

While we were feeding our faces inside, the bus filled up with smoke. By the grace of God, Shannon woke up, bolted out of the bus, and came running to me. With tears in her eyes, she said she wasn't sure how much longer she could keep living like "one of the guys." The good news is, thanks to her smoke-filled experience, we realized the time had come to get a nicer bus—one with carpet, seats, and even heat!

On another run, we had to drive across the country—from Washington, DC, to California. We had to be in Los Angeles by a specific time. But Shannon hadn't seen the Grand Canyon before, so we checked the map and saw that we could route the trip through that part of Arizona and still make it to LA on time. When we got to the canyon, we slipped the transmission into neutral, stuck our heads out the windows, took a few quick pictures, and then kept on going. (Cue Willie Nelson's theme song.) If there's a world record for shortest visit to the Grand Canyon, surely our four-second drive-by would beat it! *Technically*, Shannon got to see the Grand Canyon, but sadly there was no time to stop and take in the majestic view.

I will always be thankful for God's infinite grace and mercy that allowed me the privilege of marrying my childhood sweetheart. After the horrible abuse I had experienced in my life, after Dad's cancer and death, after dreams dying and being reborn, I thank and praise Him for truly saving the best for last and allowing me the blessing of walking through life with my best friend.

> O LORD, you have examined my heart
> > and know everything about me.
> You know when I sit down or stand up.
> > You know my thoughts even when I'm far away.
> You see me when I travel
> > and when I rest at home.
> > You know everything I do.
> You know what I am going to say
> > even before I say it, LORD.
> You go before me and follow me.
> > You place your hand of blessing on my head.
> Such knowledge is too wonderful for me,
> > too great for me to understand! (Psalm 139:1–6 NLT)

Nine

EVERYTHING IMPOSSIBLE

I was taught to be practical in everything I do,
Holding on to what is tangible,
And then came You,
That's when I found myself so far away, from
everything I knew.
— MercyMe, "Everything Impossible,"
from *Undone* (2004)*

I was now a married man, making music on the road, traveling with my new bride and my band buddies. There's a scene in *I Can Only Imagine* where the guys ask if we are still a band, and I answer, "No. We're a family." That was the absolute truth for me back then, and it still is today.

Dad had died seven years earlier. From the moment Mammaw Millard said to me as we were driving away from the graveside, "I

---

* Words and music by MercyMe and Peter Kipley. Copyright © 2004 Simpleville Music (ASCAP), Wet As A Fish Music (ASCAP) and Wordspring Music LLC / Songs From The Indigo Room (SESAC). All rights reserved. Used by permission.

127

can only imagine what Bub must be seeing right now," I had not been able to get those first four words, that phrase, out of my mind. "I can only imagine" frequently popped into my head whenever I thought about the awe and wonders of heaven and seeing Jesus for the first time.

I doodled those words on everything. The concept consumed me. Whether I was sitting in a meeting with Rusty talking about student ministry, on the road with the band and on the phone with Shannon, or sitting in a church service with my journal—if I had a pen and paper in my hand, I scribbled down that phrase.

A Lifetime in Ten Minutes

When we moved back to Texas, MercyMe was gaining momentum as a band but still working independent of any record label, manager, or agency, just as we had from the start. As we had vowed, we stayed completely out of the Christian music industry altogether. We worked hard to stay in God's will—and to pay the bills. We traveled full-time, playing churches and conferences every weekend, and our summers were filled with leading worship at weeklong youth camps. After that showcase night in Nashville, our concerts focused heavily on praise and worship but with a rock and pop sound.

We had recorded *Traces of Rain* in 1996, right before we left Oklahoma for Nashville, and then—just when you thought it couldn't get any better or wetter—released *Traces of Rain, Volume II* in 1997, having recorded that project right after we moved from Nashville to Dallas. Both of those projects were our versions of other people's popular worship songs—covers, as they are called. Even in my high school years, I knew I wanted to be involved with guys who, together, would create and play original music. As a band, we were so ready to write and record our own music because our goal was to lead people into God's presence using songs we had written.

We wanted to cut our next record—our fifth independent release—as soon as possible. We decided to call it *The Worship Project*, and it would turn out to be the game changer for us.

Late one night we were on the bus, headed back home to Texas after leading worship at a student conference all weekend. The next morning we were going to begin one final day of recording, but we still wanted one more song for the project. I told the guys I wanted to work on some lyrics, so they agreed to let me skip my driving shift to write, which was a big deal. Taking your designated shift was mandatory.

Looking for a clean page, I thumbed through the journal where I wrote down new ideas. I kept coming across where I had written "I can only imagine." It was *everywhere*. I hadn't realized how much I had jotted down those words.

In that moment, I finally saw the phrase so clearly. As in my moment of realization with Shannon, the words had been there all along, right in front of me.

Now the timing—God's timing—was right for this new song to be born.

I found a brand-new page and grabbed a pen. As fast as I could write, the words came.

> *I can only imagine what it will be like*
> *When I walk, by Your side*
> *I can only imagine what my eyes will see*
> *When Your face is before me*
> *I can only imagine*
> *I can only imagine*

Surrounded by Your glory
What will my heart feel
Will I dance for You Jesus
Or in awe of You be still
Will I stand in Your presence
Or to my knees will I fall
Will I sing hallelujah
Will I be able to speak at all
I can only imagine
I can only imagine
I can only imagine when that day comes
When I find myself standing in the Son
I can only imagine when all I would do is forever
Forever worship You
I can only imagine
I can only imagine†

I wrote the lyrics just like that, the very first time, as they were on the original recording, as they still are today. No tweaks. No changes.

That was the only time in my history of writing that I've written a song, start to finish, in ten minutes. I've heard such stories from my musical heroes, but it had never come close to happening to me—until that moment.

After I read over the lyrics, I felt the song was right just as it was, which is not at all the norm for me, or for most songwriters I know. I was pumped.

It was now very late at night, or better said, really early in the morning. There's always been something cool about creating art, just God and me, in the stillness, when the rest of the world is fast asleep. That's when I usually do my best work.

Shannon was asleep among the guys sprawled out on the mattresses. I quietly woke her up, handed her the journal where I had scribbled out the lyrics, and asked her to read them.

Bleary-eyed, she sat up. I watched her slowly scan down the page.

I don't recall exactly what she said, but her middle-of-the-night, sleepyhead response was not the over-the-top excitement I expected to receive.

Honestly, I was a bit bummed that she didn't show more enthusiasm. I suggested she just go back to sleep, which she gladly did. I, on the other hand, was so excited that I couldn't sleep the rest of the night. (Shannon responded much better when she read them again the next morning, when she was wide awake.)

Shannon's Side of the Story

"Bart woke me up in the middle of the night and told me he wanted me to look at a new song he had just written. I could tell he was excited. But waking me up to read song lyrics wasn't that unusual for Bart. I scanned down the page at the very moving words. When I got to the end, I knew the significance of the song right away. I told him I thought it was really special.

"Now, when you wake a girl up in the middle of the night, expecting some amazing response from her just isn't very fair. Give me another shot in the morning after a cup of coffee and things will be different, I promise! Which is exactly what happened. But, regardless, I will always fondly recall that memory when 'Imagine' was born as a spiritually magical moment in our lives."

From Pen to Production

When we arrived in Texas, we went straight to our makeshift studio in a Sunday school room at the church in Greenville. We had only one more day in the room before we had to clear out our gear. So as soon as we got all the equipment up and running, I showed the guys the lyrics and my idea for the melody, and we started working out the music and arrangement.

When the band jumped into the mix, it quickly became a fast rock song. That concept wasn't at all what was in my head, so I got frustrated.

"Hey, guys, let's just forget this for now," I said. "We'll work on it another time." The lyrics were so special to me, and in my super-protective state, I felt marrying them to the perfect melody was really crucial.

After a while we started breaking down our gear and packing up. Jim was still sitting at the piano, and I heard him randomly play three notes in sequence. I walked over to him and said, "Play those notes you just played again."

"You mean this?" he asked, repeating them on the keyboard.

Excitedly, I said, "That's it!" Those ended up being the first three notes you hear in the intro to the song. The melody started coming together, and I asked the guys to get their gear back out.

Over the next hour or so, the song gelled. We ended up cutting the entire song that day. So in about eighteen hours, "Imagine" went from an idea scribbled on a page to being a fully finished and recorded song.

I knew I had finally written a song, using Mammaw Millard's captivating line, about what I envisioned Dad's experience in heaven must be like, but none of us had any idea that it might have a major impact on people. So we ended up putting "Imagine" as the fifth song on *The Worship Project*. We didn't even add it into our worship set, although it was a vertical offering sung to God.

Most worship songs have a single verse and a chorus—because a second verse doesn't allow the song to fit on a single PowerPoint slide. One of MercyMe's inside jokes has always been "Is it a 7–11 song?"—in other words, is it a song with a seven-word chorus that you can sing eleven times? Worship songs have always had a simpler structure than typical songs, so they are easy to sing along with. In contrast, "Imagine" had the regular song pattern of two verses and a bridge with a repeated chorus.

So for a long time, "Imagine" was almost a secret. The song got *zero* attention from us or anyone else. Looking back now, it would have been so easy for it to stay hidden in the middle of that little independent record and never see the light of day. But God had another plan, for sure, far beyond what we would have ever dreamed possible.

A Random Request

When God wants something to happen, He always makes a way. I believe we call those *miracles*. Here is one of ours.

In 2000, we were leading worship at a youth camp when someone asked us if we would play "Imagine" during the altar call. *What? "Imagine"?* The request took the entire band by surprise.

We had never done the song live before, and we had never had anyone request that we play it. We always worked hard to accommodate the people where we served, so while the event's speaker was preaching the message, we were backstage, going over everyone's parts. We were learning how to play the song live literally half an hour before we went out to perform it.

The preacher set up the invitation, and for the first time, we played "Imagine" in front of an audience. As the song ended, we all thought we had really blown it. Because of the bright stage lights, we couldn't see the crowd's reaction, and we were confused as to why it was so quiet. But just then, the house lights came up a bit, and, after our eyes adjusted, we saw the altar was covered with people who were on their knees, crying and embracing one another.

We thought *nothing* had happened, but *something* definitely had. The Lord had used the song to touch people in a unique way. That was the genesis moment—the start of God using "Imagine" time and time again in countless situations all over the world.

Almost from that moment, the song began gaining traction. Because of the strong response, we started singing "Imagine" at every event—and things began to change.

Before releasing *The Worship Project*, if we sold a thousand CDs in a year, we thought we were doing amazing. But that next year, because of the popularity of the song, we sold 130,000. I had seen an interview with MC Hammer where he said that if you sell 100,000 CDs out of the trunk of your car at your shows, it was the same as selling a million while on a record label. For obvious reasons, I latched on to that comment.

Now our audience was growing, and we started getting more and more attention. Bigger, more-established bands heard us at youth conferences and told their record labels to check us out. We made enough money to put everyone on salary, including health insurance. We even started our own 401(k)s. Believe me—those are highly unusual financial feats for any band.

At the same time, our growth became overwhelming behind the scenes. We struggled to keep up with booking, management, publicity, CD and merchandise inventory, and marketing. Add traveling, playing more than two hundred dates a year, writing, and recording—we found ourselves weighed down with all the work that goes into keeping a band afloat aside from the two hours onstage every night. There was no relief in sight.

Our old friend Brickell found out about "Imagine" and listened to it. And then he listened again. And again. Then he made a phone call to Mark Stuart of Audio A.

Mark came to Brickell's office, lay down on the floor with headphones on—in his classic laid-back, Stuart style—and listened to the track. Brickell watched him for a response, any response.

Mark's eyes were closed; he was into it. When the song ended, he sat there a moment before asking, "Bart wrote this?"

"He did."

Mark just smiled, shook his head in a go-figure fashion, and said, "This is really an amazing song."

Brickell laughed. "I know. I can't stop listening to it."

Mark decided that he would make it his mission to get our band signed to a record label. True to his word, with Brickell's watchful guidance, he went to all the major labels—and got turned down.

For MercyMe, this was just the same song, second verse. We had been down this road before; now a major artist and manager were going to bat for us, and still nothing was connecting. But in a plot twist that none of us could see coming, God had something waiting right around the corner.

Providential Phone Call #1

MercyMe was in Des Moines, Iowa, leading worship at a weekend student conference. At the time, we had a band cell phone that we all shared. During a break at the event, our phone rang. I saw it was a 615 area code, so I knew it was a Nashville number. When I answered, the woman on the other end said, "Is this Bart Millard? Hey, this is Amy Grant."

I laughed. This had to be a joke by one of my prankster friends—probably one of the guys in the band getting me back for something I had pulled in the past. So I promptly hung up.

And then the cell rang again. Same number.

In that heart-racing moment, I thought, *Oh, man, I might have actually just laughed at and hung up on my hero.*

I answered, and Amy quickly said, "Bart, it's really me, Amy Grant—don't hang up! Hey, I heard your song, and I love it. I really want to record it, release it as a single to radio, and put it on my next album."

I was completely shocked. "I appreciate this so much," I said, "but I'll need to talk this over with the band. I will call you back as soon as possible."

When I told the guys that Amy Grant wanted to record "Imagine," they didn't believe me at all. Like me, they thought it was a prank or a joke. And given my track record, who could blame them? Finally, I showed them the number on the phone, and they started freaking out as much as I was.

We all saw, time and time again, the truth in Proverbs 19:21: "You can make many plans, but the LORD's purpose will prevail" (NLT). We get lots of phone calls in our lives, but only a handful of those are life changing. That one was particularly special to me because it had God's fingerprints all over it. Amy Grant, the queen of CCM—the singer who, with her angelic voice and words of peaceful comfort, had gotten me through so many moments of pain when I was younger—called Bart Millard, the kid from Greenville, Texas, who sings in a little indie worship band. Her music had been a major lifeline for me when I was a kid, and she was now going to record my song—my *dad's* song.

The band had told me that the decision regarding the song was up to me since I was the sole writer. But honestly, I never thought twice about signing "Imagine" over to her. We had already released another independent album titled *Look* that we were busy promoting. And *anything* Amy records is going to do well and travel far, given how many of her songs are now part of classic CCM history.

As the news of Amy's offer got out around Nashville, guess what happened? The same Christian labels that had turned us down at least twice before started calling. "Hey, we heard Amy is cutting one of your songs," they'd say. "We need to talk to you guys again."

Providential Phone Call #2

By this time, Shannon and I were shipping MercyMe product from our garage to around four hundred Christian bookstores. The increased interest in the band and the calls from labels in Nashville only added to our exhaustion. We were doing *everything* ourselves, and I knew it was time to get some help.

I called Mark Maxwell, a music lawyer we had gotten to know when we were in Nashville. I knew he believed in MercyMe. I told him everything that was going on and explained that we desperately needed help. He suggested I call a respected guy in the CCM industry named Jeff Moseley. Mark was clear that Jeff would likely turn us down—he dealt with much bigger artists—but he said I should start with him as the best first try.

We did a little checking and found out that Jeff had been in Christian music for more than twenty years and had held the positions of general manager of Myrrh Records and president of Reunion Records, Star Song Records, and Benson Records. He had been at the helm of several major Christian labels and in charge of many high-profile and bestselling projects.

But Jeff was growing weary of the traditional model and was ready to do something unique. In 1999 he started his own label, working with established artists, which is exactly why Mark figured he wouldn't talk to us. What no one else knew was that Jeff was looking for new, unsigned artists who were already walking out their calling from God, and who wanted to be in a partnership with a label, not just have someone dictate what they did in their careers. We wanted to maintain creative control and pay for our projects ourselves, and we wanted a label to come alongside us to focus on what they do best—radio promotion, marketing to the masses, and distribution to the stores.

Providential Phone Call #3

To my surprise, I got through to Jeff on the first try. I told him what we were hoping to find in a label. He told me that he was on another line and needed to put me on hold for a minute to wrap up the other call. The reason that little detail is important is that he was on a call with his wife, and—right as I was calling in—he had asked her to pray that God would bring him clarity on his new venture "even if He has to call me on the phone Himself." (That's *so* God, right?)

He came back on the line and asked me to tell him the entire MercyMe story. I told him everything, including our Christian bookstore sales numbers. Later he called about fifty stores and verified the numbers I gave him. Everything checked out.

Jeff and I talked on a Thursday, and I FedExed him *The Worship Project* CD for a Friday-morning delivery. I included a note about two or three songs for him to focus on. As he played "Imagine" for his wife that weekend, he told her, "I want to sign this band, and I think we're going to need to take out a second mortgage on our house to fund this. Are you okay with that?" She agreed, and he booked a flight to Texas for Tuesday.

With the entire band sitting in my living room and listening intently, Jeff explained the vision for his label and how we could work together. If we'd had any doubts before, they were gone now. He removed every downside of us signing with him.

We had found the perfect fit with a record label. It all made sense to everyone. Had we signed a multiyear deal with any of those other companies, this would never have happened. God connected the dots for us once again.

Jeff told us if we were going to have a record deal with his company, we would need to have an official manager who knew all the aspects of the industry well—someone who would provide oversight and creative focus, put legs to our dreams, and represent all aspects of the business end of our careers. (As Brickell always says, "Managing artists is a lot like herding cats.") Jeff had no idea that an established veteran like Brickell had been helping us and that he already had a seat on our bus, so to speak. We called Brickell right away to tell him about Jeff's plan—and he was ready.

So in 2001, seven years after our mountaintop-call-from-God moment in the Swiss Alps, we signed our first record contract with newly formed INO Records (known as Fair Trade Services today), with Jeff Moseley running point. We also signed a management agreement with the guy who had already served us so graciously for free for so many years. Brickell hit the ground running and connected us with Mike and Lisa Snider at Third Coast Artist Agency to handle all the booking of our tours and live events. A great agency with a network of relationships can put your band into places you could never book yourself. At that time, TCAA's major acts were Skillet, Caedmon's Call, and Bebo Norman, so we were excited and humbled to be on their roster.

In His way and in His timing, God had now put all the pieces in place for MercyMe to make the best music we could with the best team on the planet. More than fifteen years later, we're still with the same key people—Brickell, Jeff, and Mike. That's an anomaly in the music business. But God specializes in creating those, doesn't He?

Small World, Big God

Several years after we had been working with Brickell, we were all hanging out and started swapping back-in-the-day stories about other CCM artists. I told one from when I was in junior high, around the same time Dad had checked out on me and told me he no longer cared what I did. I had entered a local singing contest, and the winner got to sing one song as the opener for a touring Christian artist who was coming through town. The winner, along with a friend, also got to eat pizza with the singer before the show. Well, I entered, won, and took Kent with me.

The artist had a young guy with him, acting as road manager, who was carrying his gear, setting up, and running sound. During dinner, Kent and I quietly made fun of the artist's latest album title, because we thought it was really cheesy. One of us would say something at normal volume, then mutter the line under our breath to each other, followed by a giggle in that annoying way that only junior high boys can. The artist was paying zero attention to us anyway.

Saying how I had made one final joke to Kent, I was building everyone in the room up to my punch line, when Brickell suddenly interrupted me.

"Then a piece of pepperoni flew across the table and hit you right in the middle of the forehead, just like David's stone hit Goliath, right?"

I was speechless and shocked, and it's hard to get me to be either.

I blurted, "Yeah! How in the world could you know that?"

Brickell just grinned in his classic possum style and said, "'Cause I was the guy who threw it at you! I heard what you both were saying about his album, and I was ready to put a stop to it. I was the road manager for that artist."

That Christian artist was Brian Becker, who we later became friends with, and we've all laughed together about this story. For the record, Brian made fun of that album too.

It is indeed a small world, is it not? Only God could have had Brickell and me unknowingly cross paths way back then, during one of the worst times of my life. Brickell was working with a touring artist, and I was opening the concert as a singer—ten years before we would meet again in exactly the same roles. But the next time, no flying pepperoni was involved.

Ten

KEEP SINGING

But when I am stuck and I can't move,
When I don't know what I should do,
When I wonder if I will make it through,
I gotta keep singing, I gotta keep praising Your name.
—MercyMe, "Keep Singing,"
from *Undone* (2004)*

With Jeff at INO Records now in the mix, we decided that Amy would press on with recording "Imagine," but we would also put it on our first major-label release. Then, when Amy sent the song to Christian radio, we would simultaneously send our first single—a different song—spinning it as a new release "from the band that brought you Amy Grant's hit song 'I Can Only Imagine.'"

There was just one glitch with this plan. It was exactly that— *our* plan. When you are dealing with major-league, legendary-level,

---

high-demand artists who have a big machine behind them, *everything* moves slowly. Very slowly. MercyMe had once written, recorded, and released two albums in one year, so we were accustomed to knocking things out—or kicking butt and taking names, as we say in Texas. We learned the hard way that is not reality in the world of professional music.

An Afternoon with Amy

While we were sitting impatiently in the music industry's metaphorical waiting room, Amy called and offered to fly Shannon and me to Nashville to visit with her and her record producer, Brown Bannister, in the recording studio where "Imagine" was being cut. I was a huge fan of Brown's work, as I had listened to all the artists whose projects he had produced over the years. Bottom line, I was going to have the privilege of sitting down with *two* of my musical heroes.

Shannon and I flew into Nashville, and Brickell picked us up at the airport. We drove to Franklin, a historic suburb just south of the city. Amy's project was being produced in the famous Sound Kitchen studio, where so many amazing Christian albums—ones I had owned and listened to countless times—have been recorded.

Amy wasn't there when we arrived, but Brown wanted to go ahead and play me the track so I could hear what had been recorded to get an idea of the song's sound. He hit Play, and from out of the studio's mega-speakers, this huge, anthem-like version of "Imagine" roared into the room. By the time the final note faded away, I was in absolute awe.

Brown said, "You'll have to forgive me for the track still being kind of bare. The London Symphony Orchestra hasn't been added yet."

I had no idea how to respond, but I was thinking, *What am I doing here, and what is happening right now?* Let's just say that Brown's track sounded way better than anything we had produced in the day-care center in Oklahoma City or in the Sunday school room in Texas. (If this were a text, I'd insert the crying-laughing emoji here.)

By that point, Amy had slipped into the room and was standing behind us. Brown smiled, and I knew that *she* must be here. I turned around to face Amy and her manager, Jennifer Cooke.

I was starstruck, dumbfounded, and any other word for "out of my mind" you want to insert here. I think I said something like, "You're Bart and I'm Miss Amy. . . . No, wait, I'm sorry. Well . . . you know who you are. . . . I'm Bart and this is my wife, Shannon."

Amy's calm demeanor put me at ease quickly. After a few minutes, I became relatively normal again and was able to speak somewhat intelligibly.

Brown, Brickell, and Jennifer graciously excused themselves into another room and left Amy to visit with Shannon and me in the studio's control room. As we talked, Amy told me for the first time how she had heard "Imagine."

"Jennifer had a dear friend who was very ill in the hospital. The friend told her that she had to hear this amazing song. When she listened to 'Imagine,' she thought that it would be perfect for me. She put the CD into my car stereo system so it would play when I got in. After I heard it, I called Jennifer in tears. I told her how I had already played it at least fifty times. Then I asked her, 'Where in the world did this song come from?'"

Amy then paused and asked me, "Bart, where *did* this song come from?"

I swallowed hard. "You know, I've never told anybody my story. . . . My dad was a monster. I mean, that's the only word for it.

And I saw God transform him from the man I hated into the man I wanted to become, into my best friend. This song was born out of that experience. It took me about ten minutes to write it late one night on the bus."

She smiled sweetly, leaned in toward me, and said, "Bart, you didn't write this song in ten minutes. It took a lifetime."

She continued, "This song is a career maker, and I know some songs can be really personal to the writer. Is that what you really want? To allow someone else to record your song and tell your story?"

This generous question showed Amy's character and wisdom. She knew whoever released "Imagine" would, from that point forward, be connected to its message. And she was asking me, face-to-face, if I was okay with what was actually my story being forever associated with her.

"I want as many people as possible to hear it. You can do that. We can't," I said. "So, yes, this is what I want."

When we had finished talking and everyone came back into the control room, Amy looked at Brown and then back at me. She laughed and said, "Well, Bart, it's time for me to start the vocals, and I would prefer to *not* sing them in front of you."

I laughed, too, knowing what it feels like for a vocalist to sing in front of the songwriter. We hugged, and Shannon and I said our goodbyes.

Grace and Favor

A year later, we had finished our first INO full-length album, *Almost There*, but Amy still hadn't released "Imagine." The band, Brickell, and Jeff all knew we needed to send a song to radio. Every evangelical church in America was reading and talking about a

Christian book based on the prayer of Jabez from 1 Chronicles 4, so we wrote and recorded a song called "Bless Me Indeed (Jabez's Song)." This became our first official radio single.

While it might have sounded like a good idea on paper to ride the coattails of the book's momentum, the song absolutely tanked. Very few stations played it, and our record sales started dropping. Needless to say, things were not going according to plan. In football language, we were behind in the fourth quarter, it was fourth down with no time-outs left, and only seconds remained on the clock.

Jeff was about to send out our second single to radio, but he asked if someone would contact Amy's team one last time to see if they were still planning to release "Imagine." Brickell put in the call. At 5:15 p.m. that same day, her team responded to him with a message from Amy herself.

Amy had heard about the band's dilemma. She said she knew how a song could change everything in a musician's career, and how an artist could spend a lifetime trying to come up with a song like this, but we had already done it. Amy assured us that "Imagine" was ours, not hers, and she would sign the recording rights back to us.

Who does that in the entertainment industry, much less in the music business?

Brickell called us immediately and told us about Amy's blessing. When I found out, I called her myself.

"Bart, you need to finish what you started," she said. "This is your story. It's your song. You guys need to release it as your own single."

Brickell called Jeff right away to stop the new single from being mailed out. Jeff was, of course, ecstatic about the news. He had wanted to send out the song as the band's single all along, and now it was finally going to happen. (Remember that second mortgage he had taken out?) His team took off in a mad dash. They unpacked the old CDs, burned "Imagine" onto new ones, repackaged them, and drove to the FedEx center at the Nashville airport, arriving just before the planes left.

Meanwhile, I got on the phone in the middle of the night and left messages on radio station answering machines to say our new single was coming on Monday. It was a whirlwind weekend.

"Imagine" reached radio stations on October 12, 2001. The first week, thirteen stations added it to their playlists. Nineteen more added it the second week and nine more the week after. Within a month, forty-one of the top forty-three stations were playing the song. Just as Brickell, Jeff, Amy, Jennifer, and Mark Stuart all knew would happen, Christian radio programmers loved the song and started playing it in heavy rotation. (That's radio lingo for "all the stinkin' time.")

Milestone Moments

In early January 2002, I was scheduled to call in for a live interview with Jon Rivers, the legendary host of *20: The Countdown Magazine*, a nationwide syndicated radio program that counted down the top twenty songs in Christian music each week. Jon always had a special guest artist on the show for each broadcast, and he had invited me on.

While I was on hold, waiting for Jon to come on the line, I held my sleeping newborn son, Sam, born on January 4, in my arms. Shannon walked in from getting the mail, holding out a specific envelope toward me. It was the final six-hundred-dollar check from my dad's pension. The last one. All those years, and this was the end of the road.

Six hundred dollars represented a lot of money in our monthly budget. Fear gripped my heart. *What am I going to do? How can I possibly replace that income? I have a newborn son!* I thought. *Lord, help*, I prayed.

Jon picked up the phone to start the interview, jarring me out of my financial panic. In his stellar radio voice, he said, "Well, Bart, so many of us know the story of you writing 'Imagine' about your dad's death. How proud do you think he would be with the big news today? What do you think he might say to you?"

I had no idea what he meant, no clue what he was referring to. "I'm sorry. I don't think I know what you mean."

Jon laughed. "Well, then let me be the first to congratulate you! This morning 'I Can Only Imagine' hit number one at Christian radio all across the country! You have the number one song in all of Christian music!"

There, on live radio, I started to weep. I couldn't believe it. I remembered how, when Dad told me about the pension, he'd said, "I don't know what will happen after ten years, but I'm sure I will find a way to keep taking care of you."

On the *very* day that the last check arrived, the song I wrote— about Dad and for Dad—went to number one! He had indeed found a way to keep taking care of his son. Right on time, on the exact day, at just the perfect moment, as I held his grandson in my arms.

No one can write better scripts than God.

Everyone in the Christian music industry had known about Amy's plan to release "Imagine" as her first single on her new album. But we had released the song as our own, and it had gone to number one on the Christian charts.

Amy had scheduled a major concert at the Ryman Auditorium in Nashville during Gospel Music Association Week in April. Back then the event culminated with the Dove Awards, which is kind of like the Christian Grammys, on the week before Easter Sunday. So many people were asking questions about the song and why we were releasing it instead of Amy, so Brickell called to work out a plan with her team. We wanted to show how everyone had worked together toward the decision.

At the concert, Amy shared how "Imagine" had affected her. She said that she loved it but realized the song needed to be sung by the writer who had lived the story. She did an amazing job of explaining why the song was first being released by us, and then later, in a slightly different version, by her on her upcoming *Hymns* album.

Then came that surreal moment when I took the stage to sing the second verse and finish out the song with her.

For many years, MercyMe had worked so hard to make it as a band and to be well-known and respected artists in our own right. Since I was a kid, I had been Christian music's biggest fan, and now I was sharing in the legacy of my beloved music.

MercyMe was still relatively unknown at that point, so the media was all over me for comments afterward. They had no idea who I was. Years later, someone who was there that night told me he had never seen a grin as big as the one I was wearing.

But later that night, once everything had had a chance to sink in, I wept with the realization that, for the first time I could remember, life was better than anything I had ever dreamed in my imagination.

At the Dove Awards later that week, "Imagine" won Song of the Year and Pop/Contemporary Recorded Song of the Year. I was humbled and honored to also win Songwriter of the Year. It is still so ironic to me that I have worked so many long hours on so many songs but won that coveted award for the song I wrote the fastest.

The Song That Won't Go Away

"Imagine" had stayed at number one on Christian radio for weeks in 2002. Then one morning in 2003, someone called in to a mainstream FM radio station in Dallas and dared the DJ to play "Imagine." The station aired a popular morning program called

The Fitz Show whose on-air personality often played a truth-or-dare-type game on-air. Callers would challenge him to do random, sometimes crude, things.

Once the caller explained what the song was about, the DJ said, "Not just no, but *no way!*" But one of the producers at the station "just so happened" to be a Christian who was attending seminary to prepare for the ministry. He later told me that he believed God had brought him to that station to make a difference. The producer got the song and urged the DJ to play it. He finally agreed to do so as a joke for his listeners.

A friend called to tell me about this mainstream station playing "Imagine" right at that moment. I thought it had to be a prank, or else my friend had to be wrong about what he heard. I was at home, so I turned on the radio and tuned the dial to 100.3.

The DJ was telling people to please stop calling—they would play the song again later. I couldn't believe it. This was for real!

The rest of the morning show was dedicated to playing "Imagine." People called in to talk about what the words meant to them and how it made them feel. The DJ even said at one point, "What is the deal with this song?" The phones just kept ringing with people asking what the name of the band was and how to get the song.

The station also had a weekly online popularity contest that gave listeners the opportunity to vote for their favorite song. The next week "Imagine" went to number one at that station and stayed there for several months, winning out over all the mainstream pop songs of the day. Can you believe a song about Jesus and heaven beat out songs about partying and clubbing?

The DJ said that he had been told that MercyMe lived in the Dallas area. "So, Bart, if you're listening, please call us." So I phoned in, and he invited the band to be on the show.

In an interview around that time, Jeff Moseley, the head of

INO, talked about the mainstream attention, saying, "It was a surprise, and it wasn't. We have felt for a long time like there was more to 'Imagine' than the long run at Christian radio. We thought it could make an impact at mainstream. At the same time, we recognized that we couldn't do it ourselves. *Something* was going to have to make it happen." Well, that *something* certainly did occur in a way no one would ever have dreamed up.

I kept thinking that if there were a list titled "Top Five Christian Songs That Were Never Meant to Cross Over to Mainstream," I would have for sure put "Imagine" down as one of them. After all, it came complete with the J-word in the lyrics—something rarely done in secular media—and the message was so blatantly and unapologetically Christian.

Other mainstream stations around the country heard about the song's success in the Dallas market and started to play it. A representative of Curb Records called Jeff and said they wanted to help get the song out to a broader audience, so our label partnered with them. They sent it out to every reporting radio station in the country, with a simple, singular printed message: "Play it once. If you get a response, great; if you don't, throw it away."

The song went to number one in virtually every market where it was played.

One programmer reported, "I heard 'Imagine' on another station and decided to play it. The first time, I gave no introduction or announcement, and I immediately started getting calls and e-mails from people about the song." Another said, "'Imagine' is the first song with a blatant Christian message that we've added in sixteen years."

When asked about the mainstream attention, I always said that, unless somebody has a vendetta against God, the song is not a threat to anyone, believer or not. It just makes you ask a lot of questions like, "What's next after this life?" and "What if this heaven place is real?" We had the incredible privilege of assuring people that we believe it is. The world is our mission field, and MercyMe's fans have always supported us by praying that we will maintain the message and make a difference for the kingdom of God.

We had released our major label project called *Spoken For* in 2002, and everyone on our team had been busy promoting it. When mainstream radio blew up, we had to switch gears and go back to work on *Almost There* because of all the sudden attention "Imagine" was getting. That season was full of a ton of hard work, but it was an amazing time. We led worship at a Christian conference and then flew to Los Angeles to be on Ryan Seacrest's radio show. We played a denominational conference in an arena and then played *The Tonight Show with Jay Leno*. Having a hit on Christian *and* mainstream stations produces some really interesting opportunities.

Here are a few stats to put into perspective what had happened:

- *Almost There* released in August 2001 and was certified Gold (half a million in sales) within ten months.
- Our second album, *Spoken For*, was released three months later.
- Our first single, also titled "Spoken For," went to number one on Christian radio.
- Our second single, "Word of God Speak," went to number one on Christian radio.
- *Almost There* was certified Platinum (one million in sales) in July 2003.
- *Spoken For* was certified Gold in October 2003.
- "Word of God Speak," from the *Spoken For* album, won the Dove Award for Song of the Year in 2004.

After the mainstream radio miracle occurred, *Almost There* sold another one million records. And, as developing technology changed the way we buy music, "Imagine" became the first Christian song to reach two million downloads sold. In December 2017, *Almost There* was certified as Triple Platinum (sales of three million), making MercyMe only the second Christian artist in history to reach this milestone, behind our friend Amy Grant.

It is absolutely crazy to me that as I write this, seventeen years after its debut, "Imagine" just hit number one yet again on the iTunes Christian chart. Only God could have orchestrated such a miraculous way to have millions of people hear about heaven and their own opportunity to see Jesus face-to-face. We won't know until Christ returns how many people have been affected by such a simple song based on a phrase from my Mammaw Millard.

In every interview about the song I've ever done, I've told the story about my dad. "Imagine" is an ongoing tribute to my heavenly Father and to my earthly father. Dad always told me he would be forgotten soon after he was gone, but his attachment to this song has kept his story alive. What a legacy!

MercyMe's prayer has always been that God would use us in this generation as He did the biblical psalmists in theirs. What an immense privilege to think that a song we wrote might outlive the band. We just want to lead people to the throne of God through celebration, worship, and praise. We were doing this long before worship music became commercial, and we want to keep doing it as long as the Lord allows and calls us to lead. Why shouldn't we? That is the very reason we were created!

Looking back on my life, through all the faith and fear, victories and failures, mountains and valleys, this one thing I know, just like the song says: *Lord Jesus, I will forever, forever worship You.*

CONCLUSION

Even If

They say it only takes a little faith to move a
mountain,
Well, good thing,
A little faith is all I have right now,
But God, when You choose to leave mountains
unmovable,
Give me the strength to be able to sing,
It is well with my soul.
—MERCYME, "EVEN IF," FROM *LIFER* (2017)*

Let's get real: I can see how it would be easy for you to read about the hit songs, awards, celebrities, and spotlights on stages all over the country, and then do the math on selling millions of records. You could quickly come to the conclusion that my early years were

---

* Words and music by MercyMe, Tim Timmons, Crystal Lewis, David Garcia, and Ben Glover. Copyright © 2017 Tunes of MercyMe (SESAC), Letsbebeautiful / All Essential Music (ASCAP), Crystalized (ASCAP), and D Soul Music / Universal Music - Brentwood Benson Publishing / 9t One Songs / Ariose Music (ASCAP). All rights reserved. Used by permission.

really tough, but then the metaphorical yellow brick road led me to the classic storybook ending. From that point on, life was all unicorns and rainbows, right?

It was really tempting to end the book with the previous chapter: "Imagine" went to number one, and we all lived happily ever after. *The end. Goodnight! God bless you! Thanks for coming! We'll see you next time we're in town!*

As I mentioned up front, the movie was forced to tell my story in under two hours because that's the nature of the format. But here, I've had time to kick back and dig into the details. You've been able to put a bookmark in my life and jump back in when you wanted. But if we are going to be honest about following Christ, we have to talk about the doubts with the faith, the questions with the answers, and the trials with the triumphs. So let's pull back the curtain and go backstage. Get on the bus, Gus. Let me tell you about my life in 2004 and 2005, following the controlled chaos of 2002 and 2003. While MercyMe was experiencing the *best* year ever as a band, I was going through the *worst* year of my personal life.

When you have the biggest hit song in history in your musical genre, the pressure from the industry is unbelievable, almost unbearable. Everyone expected another power ballad to match or even rival "Imagine."

How in the world do you top that? *Can* you top that? Especially when it was so obviously a work of the Lord. You don't just send up a prayer and schedule those into your life. That's why they call it *God's will.*

Just don't ruin what we've got became MercyMe's unspoken motto. That attitude permeated the band's being. We were working so hard just to not derail the momentum that the hit song had built.

When you start buying into the hype, taking on other people's pressures and expectations, and working from such a negative perspective, you can't possibly enjoy what you're doing. And you also can't try anything new and venture into fresh territory, because the past is always banging on your front door.

We were just a little worship band from Texas that wanted to make music and honor the Lord, but now everything we dreamed of and hoped for had come true. At the same time, life got really, really complicated.

Life Before and After 2004

For Shannon and me, 2004 was one of those eternal time markers. We actually refer to our lives as pre-2004 and post-2004. Late one January night, Shannon's nineteen-year-old brother, Chris, showed up at our door in Greenville—we had moved back to our home-town in 1998—and said he really needed to talk to us. He had just had his heart broken, and he was distraught.

Shannon had been his champion, no matter what, and she had always supported and believed in him. So we talked with him for hours, into the middle of the night. But he started getting rude with her, and I told him someone ought to take him outside and knock some sense into him. He asked me if I was going to be the one to do that. I clarified that I was just trying to say he desperately needed to straighten up and think through his life.

Soon after, he headed toward the front door. He opened it, stopped, and turned to us.

"Tell Sam I love him," he said. (Sam was two years old.)

We tried to get him to stay, but he refused.

It didn't take long for Shannon to get concerned about what he had said and how he had said it. She asked me to try to find him. I knew where he was staying, so I drove there.

Nothing.

I went everywhere I thought he might have gone but couldn't locate him. Finally, early in the morning, I headed back home and went to bed.

At eight in the morning, our phone rang. It was Shannon's dad. After Chris left our house, he fell asleep at the wheel. The one-car accident on a local back road had been fatal.

Shannon was in hysterics. We were both devastated. When the initial shock wore off, it hit me: I had upset him. I thought, *I'm responsible for my brother-in-law's death.* No matter how much anyone tried to reassure me that I couldn't have done anything to prevent what had happened, it didn't matter. I couldn't shake it.

The guilt was unbearable. I carried that burden around with me, along with all my other ones—old and new baggage together. But this one was different—this was about someone's death. I replayed in my mind what I could have said, what I shouldn't have said, what I should have done. The loop seemed endless.

Three months later, in April 2004, Shannon got pregnant with our second child. In early November, Shannon started having contractions, but she was still six weeks away from her due date.

The doctor and nurses at the hospital determined our baby girl was indeed coming prematurely, and there was a great deal of concern because of development issues that can often affect preemies. A lot can go wrong when a birth is that early.

On November 4, 2004, Gracie Millard came into the world. By the grace of God, she and Shannon were fine, and in a few days, we took our tiny new daughter home to join our son, Sam.

Just after we got home from the hospital, I had to fly to LA to attend the American Music Awards. MercyMe had been nominated for Favorite Contemporary Inspirational Artist. Sheryl Crow was the presenter, and when she opened the envelope, she called our name. Because of the time difference between California and Texas, I didn't call Shannon until the next morning, after I had gotten to the airport.

As soon as she answered, I said, "Hey, we won, and Sheryl Crow gave us our award!"

"Something is wrong with Sam," she replied, as though she hadn't heard me. "I've taken him to his pediatrician, but as soon as you get home, we need to take him to Children's Hospital in Dallas." Sam was constantly thirsty, as if he couldn't get enough to drink. He was also very fatigued, unusually so for a toddler.

Of course, my entire focus changed. I just needed to get back home as quickly as I could.

By the time I arrived, Shannon's parents had already come to the house to take care of Gracie, and we left right away to take Sam to the hospital. My American Music Award now sat unnoticed in the floorboard of the car. Interesting how priorities can so quickly change.

After running some tests, the doctor diagnosed Sam with juvenile diabetes. I asked, "So he'll outgrow this, right? This isn't permanent?"

When he explained what Sam had is an incurable illness, my heart broke into a million pieces. *He's still just a baby,* I thought.

Nothing hurts more than when something happens to one of your kids, especially if it's something you have zero control over. Nothing in this life is more difficult than when your little boy begs, "Fix it, Daddy," and you tell him that you can't. Everything in you screams because you want more than anything to stop his suffering.

We spent the next week in the hospital, learning more than we ever wanted to know about shots, blood tests, and diet restrictions. Every day we had to give Sam four or five shots and prick his finger ten times—and he had no idea why. It was overwhelming for all of us, especially because Gracie had just come home from the hospital.

Shannon was still recovering from childbirth and taking care of a newborn, so I had to step up to the plate in learning all the details of Sam's new lifestyle. Eventually, because Sam was such an easygoing and resilient kid, he adapted, but the added responsibilities, rigid schedule, and restricted diet was a major game changer for our family, especially after years of living the unpredictable life of a musician.

An Offer I Couldn't Refuse

The next weekend the band was supposed to play in Pasadena, California, at the Rose Bowl, for what would be one of Billy Graham's last evangelical crusade appearances.

Brickell called Dr. Graham's office and explained that the band would have to cancel due to what had happened with Sam. I just couldn't leave my family for the two to three days it would take for the bus trip. The Graham folks were very understanding and accepted our regrets, but the next day, Dr. Graham's assistant called Brickell back. He wanted to make me an offer: If a private jet picked me up at 6:00 p.m. in Texas, and I could be back home by midnight, would I consider coming? He added that Dr. Graham wanted a few minutes alone with the band to pray for Sam and our family.

What could I say? Shannon and I agreed I should go.

The band and crew went on via bus as scheduled. When I arrived at the Rose Bowl that evening, we were ushered into a covered area near the platform. On the other side, a number of security personnel appeared with a group of people, and we assumed Dr. Graham had been brought up to the stage. The press immediately began to congregate in that area. But that was only a planned diversion.

Dr. Graham walked through the doorway in the stage covering. He smiled politely, introduced himself, and explained how

160

they divert attention when he needs to visit privately with someone. He spoke with us briefly, thanked us for coming, and then prayed a beautiful, personal, heartfelt prayer over Sam and our family. It was a moment I will never, ever forget.

We played our set at the crusade, and then, just as promised, I was back home with my family by midnight.

Asking the Hard Questions

When you are perceived by the public to be a celebrity, people can say really hurtful things to you. Unintentionally hurtful, maybe, but still hurtful. They may mean well, but that doesn't make it easier to hear a total stranger talk about your kid. When people asked if we had prayed for Sam's healing or they offered some other super-spiritual sentiment, the good-church-boy side of me smiled and answered, "Yes, we sure have. Thanks so much for your concern. God is good."

But dealing with so many people who talked to us about Sam's illness made me realize that those of us in high-visibility Christianity are expected to be "on" all the time, even though we—like everyone else—have moments when it's really hard to handle life. There are nights when you don't want to stand onstage and tell people that everything is going to be all right, because sometimes you aren't certain yourself. How do you tell an arena of ten thousand people who came to hear about heaven and hope that you're hurting because of your little boy's suffering and you're struggling to just hang on to your own faith? That's not the message they paid good money to hear. You're supposed to encourage them in their problems, not voice anything about your own.

Adding to our crises, Shannon's dad was having serious health issues. After a CT scan, his doctor found a grapefruit-sized tumor in his brain. The surgeon scheduled an operation right away. They told him to say his goodbyes before surgery because he might not make it through. It's so tough to pray and believe when you have to tell someone you deeply love goodbye, just in case.

Thank God that the surgeons were able to successfully remove the tumor. But we felt very much as if we had been thrown into "the valley of the shadow of death" that the psalmist referred to in Psalm 23. As much as you hate to admit it to yourself, you start to think, *Okay, God, what horrible thing are You going to allow next? What other bad news is right around the corner?*

Bart on Bart

I was raised in a fearful, performance-based environment. So when I was introduced to the Christian life and started to read the Bible, I filtered everything more through the law of the Old Testament, not the grace of the New Testament. While the reality of faith in Christ is found in a balance between them, most Christians lean toward one side or the other—law or grace.

I most definitely leaned toward following the law, keeping the rules, and towing the line. (Remember the "I don't cuss" story?) My vision statement went something like this: "Just be a good Christian, and the good you do will always outweigh the bad." Well, honestly, doesn't that sound more like a statement about karma from Hinduism or Buddhism? Far too many of us in Western, first-world Christianity think like this.

My spiritual worldview was way more dependent on *me* following the rules and doing the right thing than on *Christ* and submitting to His saving work on the cross.

The professional expectations on me were crushing. I was MercyMe's catalyst and founder, its lead singer and front man, and the writer of its biggest hit. If there was an interview scheduled, I had to be there. If one of the other guys got sick or needed to take a leave of absence, we could hire another player for a short stint, but fans and promoters don't like the lead singer being substituted, not even for a single show. If I couldn't make it, we had to cancel. In business terms, demand for me outweighed supply.

Don't get me wrong. I love my work and have never wanted to quit, but I realized that I wanted the option the other guys had to be able to take a break or miss a show.

So, let's recap: I was facing mounting artistic and industry pressure, multiple family crises, and career claustrophobia. And all the while I felt as though my walk with God was dependent on my own behavior and ability to be strong. This, my friends, is a recipe for disaster.

Finally, I couldn't take anymore.

I hit rock bottom.

I found the end of Bart Millard.

Falling into a deep, dark cavern of depression, I stopped functioning. Sitting and staring into the abyss became a regular activity.

If you were to look at MercyMe's calendar during that time, you would have said, "But, Bart, you still hit the stage, smiled at everyone, sang your heart out, and shared hope with the crowds!" Yes, I did. It's what I do. I'm a professional artist. But here's the other side of that: the road was an escape from reality for me. Performing was a major distraction because I didn't need to do much more than sing pretty. The world on the road is really small and predictable. The daily schedule is posted on the bus door, and each day looks a lot like the day before, regardless of the city you're in.

But back home, I had to be a husband and father. I had to look

163

at the chair where my brother-in-law sat right before he walked out of our lives forever. I had to look my son in the eyes, wondering why he had to have diabetes.

This is how a lot of artists—Christian or mainstream—end up having great success but losing their families. Back home there are demands and bills and diapers, while the road brings spotlights, catered dinners, and adoring fans asking for pictures and autographs. It's an illusion that lasts only as long as the success holds up.

Come-to-Jesus Meeting

The turning point came when I went to the doctor. I stepped onto his scale and saw that I weighed 370 pounds. My blood pressure and cholesterol were high. I had developed type 2 diabetes. I was experiencing sleep apnea. And, to top it all off, I was in the beginning stages of congestive heart failure.

The doctor looked at my chart and sternly stated, "Your dad died in his forties. Your grandfather died in his forties. You are headed in exactly the same direction, to the same end, if you don't change *now*.

"I know you have another major tour right around the corner, so here's what we're going to do," he continued. "This is Thursday. Next Tuesday, I am scheduling you for gastric sleeve surgery. It's a weight-loss procedure that will remove part of your stomach and restrict the amount of food you can eat. I've seen you try to lose weight, but right now time is just something you cannot afford.

"Normally, it takes me several months to get this surgery through insurance due to the requirement of counseling to emotionally prepare you for such a transformation. But because of the small window of time you have before leaving for your tour, we need to move forward. You can start counseling afterward."

There are times when someone highly credible tells you a truth definitively and assertively. While you want to scream and run out the door in full-on denial, you just know in your heart that you need to listen and obey the expert. This was most certainly one of those times.

I complied with everything he said, and it was the beginning of a new chapter for my family. Following the surgery, all the health issues the doctor discovered went away. Over time, my blood pressure returned to normal, my cholesterol stabilized, the diabetes disappeared, and, of course, I lost a lot of weight—130 pounds, to be exact.

Inside Out

When we began the counseling required for the surgery, Shannon and I agreed that, with all that had gone on in our lives, my health crisis was ultimately a good thing. We believed it was God pushing us to get the help we needed to deal with our grief and stress, which turned out to be the reason behind my massive weight gain in the first place. She knew much of what had happened with my parents, but there was also a lot I had stuffed down, hidden, and denied that the counselor helped me work through.

For example, our entire married life, I had never wanted to do the dishes. I had no problem eating from them, but when dinner was over, picking them up and washing them was a struggle. I finally shared the story about Dad breaking the plate over my head. It's still hard for me to watch that scene in the movie.

I had always struggled to sit at the dinner table with my family. That came from Dad not letting me get up until I had eaten what was on my plate. I recalled one specific incident when he made me sit at the table for six hours until I had finished some dish he had cooked that I absolutely hated.

And then there was mowing the lawn. I had taken care of Mammaw Millard's yard, but she had very little grass—mostly just gravel with weeds growing up through it. When I cut her "grass," the mower blade kicked out tiny pieces of rock. By the time I was finished, my legs were bloody from flying debris. I would cry and tell Dad how much it hurt, but he just said I needed to toughen up and take it. I hated every minute of mowing her yard because of the pain from the cuts I endured.

I had grown up in a home where I never felt safe. In fact, that house in Greenville was the place where I felt the most fear. School, church, and my friends' homes were far more secure than the place I had lived. Now, my brother-in-law's death had caused me to feel that same lack of safety and security in my own home. The fear transferred. The memories there were too painful. I had watched my father die in my childhood home and heard my brother-in-law's final words in my adult home. I just felt that home could never be a safe place.

These are just a few of the revelations that counseling brought out for me. There were many others. I realized that I had not only avoided the problematic household activities but also avoided telling Shannon why I couldn't do them. The painful details of my abuse were the elephant in the room and—as the saying goes—the only way to eat an elephant is one bite at a time. One particular counseling session lasted all day long, which was really painful but also very good. Working on yourself and looking into your heart to deal with the pain so you can be the best person you can is absolutely the healthiest decision for you and those you love.

When Shannon and I sat down for our first counseling session, the counselor looked at me and said, "Congratulations, Bart.

Because you are here and ready to work on your life, you are in the healthiest place you have ever been." That positive perspective helped me know that everything was going to be all right.

Family Matters

Almost a year to the day after Dad died, Mom's third husband, Lawrence, died from a sudden heart attack. That sent Mom into another tailspin, and she ended up moving back to the Greenville area, where she still lives. Eventually, she met Bob, who became her fourth husband.

I had long struggled with bitterness and distance from Mom. But through the counseling, I was able to come to a healthy place in our relationship. God will give us the grace to allow His redemption to come into any relationship whenever we are ready to receive His gift of forgiveness and reconciliation.

Today, Mom is a part of my family's life. She is MercyMe's number-one fan, coming to shows whenever she can. She wears our T-shirts and tells anyone who will listen how proud she is of what I have accomplished.

My brother, Stephen, struggled for many years with Dad's death. That first Christmas season, just a few weeks after Dad's passing, was especially hard. But by God's grace, Stephen's wife, Darcy, was pregnant and due with their first child. We all knew how much Dad had hoped to be around to see his grandchildren. In fact, after everyone found out about the pregnancy, Dad had specifically asked his doctor if he would live long enough to see the birth of his first grandchild. While the physician told him he believed he would be around that long, I could tell by his eyes and the way he answered he just couldn't bear to steal that hope from Dad. I didn't blame the doctor for giving Dad a reason to fight for a little more life.

While we were opening presents that Christmas, Darcy went into labor. We dropped everything and went to the hospital. On December 26, Dad's first grandchild, a beautiful daughter named Morgan, was born. It was such a bittersweet holiday.

Morgan is now twenty-five years old. Stephen and Darcy had two other children: Adam, twenty-three, and Allison, sixteen. My brother works at Qorvo, Inc., a technology company, and their family lives in our hometown of Greenville.

For Me to Live Is Christ

The biggest piece of the puzzle in reclaiming my life was getting my walk with Christ to a healthy place. If we don't deal properly with the spirit, it doesn't matter how much we change the mind and body.

Psalm 139, the chapter that the Lord had used to confirm the relationship between Shannon and me, had for many years prior held a very special meaning for me. The very first poem I ever wrote was based on this passage. But I had always struggled a bit with verse 16: "All the days ordained for me were written in your book before one of them came to be." God knew I would be abandoned by my mom and beaten by my dad. He also knew we would lose my brother-in-law and Sam would have juvenile diabetes. He allowed all that. He didn't stop it. Those are really hard concepts to grasp.

But then in the big picture, there is this . . .

Where can I go from your Spirit?
Where can I flee from your presence?

If I go up to the heavens, you are there;
    if I make my bed in the depths, you are there.
If I rise on the wings of the dawn,
    if I settle on the far side of the sea,
even there your hand will guide me,
    your right hand will hold me fast.
If I say, "Surely the darkness will hide me
    and the light become night around me,"
even the darkness will not be dark to you;
    the night will shine like the day,
        for darkness is as light to you. (vv. 7–12)

This passage has also always reminded me that God is in control, not me. No matter what we go through, no matter what life throws at us, He is there in the midst of it. He doesn't take us *out* of the valley, as we would prefer, but He is there with us *in* it.

I had to face the fact that I suffered from legalism, a spiritual disease that comes from seeing faith as a list of dos and don'ts. I was missing the lifestyle of freedom that Christ offered—that He died to give me.

I also had to face the fact that my calling to travel and lead God's people in worship had become the villain taking me away from my family. I had become out of balance, and I needed God to guide me to rediscover what He wanted of me: to reestablish the first ministry in which He had ordained me to serve. For the rest of my life, ministering to the church at-large had to become second to serving the people in my home.

Here are the new truths I came to accept about my life:

There is nothing I can possibly do for Christ to love me any more than He does right now. I grew up believing that if I could just "do my part," then God would be okay with me. I finally came to the revelation that even on my worst possible day, He is always pleased with me. My relationship with Christ has never been about *what I do* but what His work on the cross *has already done*.

> I pray that out of his glorious riches he may strengthen you with power through his Spirit in your inner being, so that Christ may dwell in your hearts through faith. And I pray that you, being rooted and established in love, may have power, together with all the Lord's holy people, to grasp how wide and long and high and deep is the love of Christ, and to know this love that surpasses knowledge—that you may be filled to the measure of all the fullness of God. (Ephesians 3:16–19)

I can make a mess of my life all day long, but I cannot mess up my relationship with Christ. To be clear, I'm not saying it is okay to sin. But when I do sin—and I most certainly will—everything is going to be okay because of my relationship with Christ. The power of sin creates a horrible wake that affects me as well as those around me. But even that cannot separate me from Christ. Even when I'm at my worst, my relationship with Christ is unchanged. He still sees me as someone He loves and adores.

> Who then will condemn us? No one—for Christ Jesus died for us and was raised to life for us, and he is sitting in the place of honor at God's right hand, pleading for us. Can anything ever separate us from Christ's love? Does it mean he no longer loves us if we have trouble or calamity, or are persecuted, or hungry, or destitute, or in danger, or threatened with death? (As the Scriptures say, "For your sake we are killed every day; we are being slaughtered like sheep.") No, despite all these things, overwhelming victory is ours through Christ, who loved us. And I am convinced

that nothing can ever separate us from God's love. Neither death nor life, neither angels nor demons, neither our fears for today nor our worries about tomorrow—not even the powers of hell can separate us from God's love. (Romans 8:34–38 NLT)

I must rest every day in Christ's finished work on the cross. My identity is not in my guilt and shame, or in the most noble of deeds I could do. My identity is sealed in what Christ has already done on the cross. Christ has chosen to offer this gift, and we must choose to receive it. Every day, I will say yes to Him as well as thank Him.

"Come to me, all you who are weary and burdened, and I will give you rest. Take my yoke upon you and learn from me, for I am gentle and humble in heart, and you will find rest for your souls." (Matthew 11:28–29)

On my absolute worst day, Christ still loves me. I am not a bad person now trying to be good. I'm just me, and Christ always loves me. My identity is wrapped up in the same Spirit that raised Christ from the dead and now lives inside of me. I can rest in the balance of knowing I live in a love that can never be broken.

Very rarely will anyone die for a righteous person, though for a good person someone might possibly dare to die. But God demonstrates his own love for us in this: While we were still sinners, Christ died for us. Since we have now been justified by his blood, how much more shall we be saved from God's wrath through him! (Romans 5:7–9)

Paul summed up the concept of grace in Romans 8:1–2: "There is now no condemnation for those who are in Christ Jesus, because through Christ Jesus the law of the Spirit who gives life has set you free from the law of sin and death."

God's grace became my new focus. I had to admit I couldn't keep the rules. I could never be good enough. I couldn't possibly keep all the boxes checked on the spiritual to-do list. Shannon and I both agreed we would stop caring so much about what anyone but the Lord thought about us. We've discovered that if we please Him, everything else gets taken care of.

My identity cannot and will not be in MercyMe, writing a hit song, or singing on a stage. My identity is found in one simple role: child of God. No matter what I do or where God calls me, my spiritual position does not change. If MercyMe ends tomorrow and I never sing again, I will still be God's son. Therefore, I will be just fine. The pressure is off. The war is won. All fear is gone. Grace truly is amazing.

> See what great love the Father has lavished on us, that we should
> be called children of God! And that is what we are! (1 John 3:1)

I have experienced God's great love firsthand. It was there in my father's transformation, in my relationship with Shannon, and in a musical career that has had an impact greater than I could ever dream of. His love was there when we faced Sam's illness and Gracie's early birth, and it was there when Shannon and I welcomed three more children: Charlie (born March 29, 2006), Sophie (born December 11, 2008), and Miles (born March 21, 2011). Even when I hit rock bottom and the mountains in front of me seemed immovable, God's love, grace, and mercy were right there.

In 2012, we moved our family of seven to Franklin, Tennessee, just outside of Nashville. We were ready to leave the difficult memories we had in Texas and make a fresh start around many of the wonderful people on our team we had gotten to know over the past ten years.

MercyMe also scaled back and cut our normal tour schedule in half to be home with our families more. The moment I realized all of my creativity and talent was simply an overflow of a healthy relationship with Christ, everything changed. We fell in love with music again, as though we were teenagers starting a garage band for the first time.

While I am here on earth, I am both a work in progress and already made whole because of the cross. I am a child of the risen King who will wrestle with the flesh. I'll win some and lose some, but it can never change how Christ sees me because the cross was enough! Even through my fears and doubts, I rest in the fact that Christ remains in me. I am living proof that He can carry you through anything. And if this is the journey I had to take to truly know Jesus and understand who I am because of His grace? Then I wouldn't change a thing.

Appendix 1

YOUR IDENTITY IN CHRIST

My mentor, Rusty Kennedy, was integral in discipling me in my walk with Christ. He gave me these seventy-five verses and statements while I was unpacking my past and starting to understand who I truly am in Jesus. Ever since then, I have carried these close to my heart. I pray these will minister to you the way they have to me so that you, too, can understand that in Christ, you are free indeed!

1. John 1:12—I am a child of God.
2. John 15:1–5—I am a part of the true vine, a channel (branch) of His life.
3. John 15:15—I am Christ's friend.
4. John 15:16—I am chosen and appointed by Christ to bear His fruit.
5. Acts 1:8—I am a personal witness of Christ for Christ.
6. Romans 3:24—I have been justified and redeemed.
7. Romans 5:1—I have been justified (completely forgiven and made righteous) and am at peace with God.
8. Romans 6:1–6—I died with Christ and died to the power of sin's rule in my life.

9. Romans 6:7—I have been freed from sin's power over me.

10. Romans 6:18—I am a slave of righteousness.

11. Romans 6:22—I am enslaved to God.

12. Romans 8:1—I am forever free from condemnation.

13. Romans 8:14–15—I am a son of God. God is literally my "Papa."

14. Romans 8:17—I am an heir of God and fellow heir with Christ.

15. Romans 11:16—I am holy.

16. Romans 15:7—Christ has accepted me.

17. 1 Corinthians 1:2—I have been sanctified.

18. 1 Corinthians 1:30—I have been placed in Christ by God's doing; Christ is now my wisdom from God, my righteousness, my sanctification, and my redemption.

19. 1 Corinthians 2:12—I have received the Spirit of God into my life that I might know the things freely given to me by God.

20. 1 Corinthians 2:16—I have been given the mind of Christ.

21. 1 Corinthians 3:16; 6:19—I am a temple (home) of God; His Spirit (His life) dwells in me.

22. 1 Corinthians 6:17—I am joined to the Lord and am one spirit with Him.

23. 1 Corinthians 6:19–20—I have been bought with a price; I am not my own; I belong to God.

24. 1 Corinthians 12:27—I am a member of Christ's body.

25. 2 Corinthians 1:21—I have been established in Christ and anointed by God.

26. 2 Corinthians 2:14—God always leads me in His triumph in Christ.

27. 2 Corinthians 5:14–15—Since I have died, I no longer live for myself but for Christ.

28. 2 Corinthians 5:17—I am a new creation.

29. 2 Corinthians 5:18–19—I am reconciled to God and am a minister of reconciliation.

30. 2 Corinthians 5:21—I am the righteousness of God in Christ.

31. Galatians 2:4—I have liberty in Christ Jesus.

32. Galatians 2:20—I have been crucified with Christ, and it is no longer I who live, but Christ who lives in me. The life I am now living is Christ's life.

33. Galatians 3:26–28—I am a child of God and one in Christ.

34. Galatians 4:6–7—I am a child of God and an heir through God.

35. Ephesians 1:1—I am a saint.

36. Ephesians 1:3—I am blessed with every spiritual blessing.

37. Ephesians 1:4—I was chosen in Christ before the foundation of the world to be holy and without blame before Him.

38. Ephesians 1:5—I have been adopted as God's child.

39. Ephesians 1:7–8—I have been redeemed and forgiven, and am a recipient of His lavish grace.

40. Ephesians 2:5—I have been made alive together with Christ.

41. Ephesians 2:6—I have been raised up and seated with Christ in heaven.

42. Ephesians 2:10—I am God's workmanship, created in Christ to do His work that He planned beforehand that I should do.

43. Ephesians 2:13—I have been brought near to God.

44. Ephesians 2:18—I have direct access to God through the Spirit.

45. Ephesians 2:19—I am a fellow citizen with the saints and a member of God's household.

46. Ephesians 3:6—I am a fellow heir, fellow member of the body, and fellow partaker of the promise in Christ Jesus.

47. Ephesians 3:12—I may approach God with boldness and confidence.
48. Ephesians 4:24—I am righteous and holy.
49. Philippians 3:20—I am a citizen of heaven.
50. Philippians 4:7—His peace guards my heart and mind.
51. Philippians 4:19—God will supply all my needs.
52. Colossians 1:13—I have been delivered from the domain of darkness and transferred to the kingdom of Christ.
53. Colossians 1:14—I have been redeemed and forgiven of all my sins. The debt against me has been canceled.
54. Colossians 1:27—Christ Himself is in me.
55. Colossians 2:7—I have been firmly rooted in Christ and am now being built up and established in Him.
56. Colossians 2:10—I have been made complete in Christ.
57. Colossians 2:12–13—I have been buried, raised, made alive with Christ, and totally forgiven.
58. Colossians 3:1—I have been raised with Christ.
59. Colossians 3:3—I have died, and my life is now hidden with Christ in God.
60. Colossians 3:4—Christ is now my life.
61. Colossians 3:12—I am chosen of God, holy, and dearly loved.
62. 1 Thessalonians 5:5—I am a child of light and not of darkness.
63. 2 Timothy 1:7—I have been given a spirit of power, love, and discipline.
64. 2 Timothy 1:9—I have been saved and called (set apart) according to God's purpose and grace.
65. Hebrews 2:11—Because I am sanctified and am one with Christ, He is not ashamed to call me His.
66. Hebrews 3:1—I am a holy partaker of a heavenly calling.
67. Hebrews 3:14—I am a partaker of Christ.

68. Hebrews 4:16—I may come boldly before the throne of God to receive mercy and find grace to help in my time of need.

69. 1 Peter 2:5—I am one of God's living stones and am being built up as a spiritual house.

70. 1 Peter 2:9-10—I am a part of a chosen race, royal priesthood, holy nation, and a people of God's own possession.

71. 1 Peter 2:11—I am an alien and stranger to this world in which I temporarily live.

72. 1 Peter 5:8—I am an enemy of the Devil. He is my adversary.

73. 2 Peter 1:4—I have been given God's precious and magnificent promises by which I am a partaker of the divine nature.

74. 1 John 3:1—God has bestowed a great love on me and called me His child.

75. 1 John 4:15—God is in me and I am in God.

Appendix 2

MERCYME CAREER OVERVIEW
Through 2017

Band Stats

Members

- Bart Millard—Lead Vocals (1994–present) 12/1/72—Greenville, TX
- Mike Scheuchzer—Guitar/Vocals (1994–present) 6/8/75—Portland, ME
- Robby Shaffer—Drums (1994–present) 11/14/75—Columbia, MO
- Nathan Cochran—Bass/Keys/Vocals (1994–present) 5/26/78—Columbia, MO
- Barry Graul—Guitar/Vocals (2003–present) 5/18/61—Baltimore, MD
- Previous Member: Jim Bryson (1994–2014)

Key Facts

- 9 million units in cumulative sales
- 57 #1 songs
- 4 mainstream radio hits

- "I Can Only Imagine" was the first digital single in Christian music history to be certified Platinum and Double Platinum.
- In 2009, Billboard named MercyMe's "Word of God Speak" the #1 Song of the Decade and the group the #1 Artist of the Decade in both the Christian Songs and Christian Adult Contemporary Songs categories.
- Notable performances include Radio City Music Hall, the Macy's Thanksgiving Day Parade, *The Today Show, CBS This Morning, The Tonight Show with Jay Leno, FOX & Friends*, CNN, and *ABC News*.
- Articles published in *Entertainment Weekly*, the *New York Times*, and *USA Today*.
- Their ninth studio album, *Lifer*, released through Fair Trade Services on March 31, 2017, reached #1 on Christian SoundScan and #10 on the Billboard Top 200 overall chart during its first week.
- The song "Even If," from the album *Lifer*, was #1 on the Billboard Christian and Mediabase Christian radio charts for a record-setting nineteen straight weeks in 2017, second only to the #1 spot held by their own song "Word of God Speak," that spent twenty-three weeks at the #1 position in 2004.
- The 2018 feature film *I Can Only Imagine* is a true story based on the life of lead singer Bart Millard and stars Dennis Quaid, Trace Adkins, J. Michael Finley, Cloris Leachman, Madeline Carroll, and Priscilla Shirer.

MercyMe Discography
- 2001 *Almost There* (RIAA Certified Triple Platinum)
- 2002 *Spoken For* (RIAA Certified Gold)

- 2004 *Undone* (RIAA Certified Gold)
- 2004 *MercyMe Live* DVD (RIAA Certified Gold)
- 2005 *The Christmas Sessions*
- 2006 *Coming Up to Breathe* (RIAA Certified Gold)
- 2007 *All That Is Within Me* (RIAA Certified Gold)
- 2009 *"10"*
- 2010 *The Generous Mr. Lovewell* (RIAA Certified Gold)
- 2011 *The Worship Sessions*
- 2012 *The Hurt & The Healer*
- 2014 *Welcome to the New* (RIAA Certified Gold)
- 2015 *MercyMe It's Christmas!*
- 2017 *Lifer*

MercyMe's #1 Radio Singles by Album*

- *Lifer*—"Even If"
- *Welcome to the New*—"Greater," "Flawless," "Dear Younger Me"
- *The Hurt & The Healer*—"The Hurt & The Healer," "You Are I Am"
- *The Generous Mr. Lovewell*—"All of Creation," "Beautiful," "Move"
- *All That Is Within Me*—"God With Us," "You Reign," "Finally Home"
- *Coming Up to Breathe*—"So Long Self," "Hold Fast," "Bring the Rain"
- *Undone*—"Here with Me," "In the Blink of an Eye," "Homesick"
- *Spoken For*—"Word of God Speak," "Spoken For"
- *Almost There*—"I Can Only Imagine"

---

* MercyMe has a total of 57 #1 singles across the following formats: National Christian Audience, Christian AC Monitored, Christian AC Indicator, Christian Soft AC, Christian AC (PD Advisor), Christian Soft AC (Radio & Records), Christian AC (Radio & Records).

MercyMe Awards and Nominations

GRAMMY Awards—Nominations

- 2015 Best Contemporary Christian Music Album—*Welcome to the New*
- 2015 Best Contemporary Christian Music Performance/Song—"Shake"

Billboard Music Awards—Nominations

- 2016 Top Christian Artist
- 2016 Top Christian Song—"Flawless"
- 2015 Top Christian Artist
- 2015 Top Christian Album—*Welcome to the New*
- 2015 Top Christian Song—"Greater"
- 2013 Top Christian Artist
- 2013 Top Christian Album—*The Hurt & The Healer*
- 2012 Top Christian Artist
- 2011 Top Christian Artist
- 2011 Top Christian Album—*The Generous Mr. Lovewell*
- 2011 Top Christian Song—"All of Creation"

American Music Awards—Wins

- 2010 Favorite Contemporary Inspirational Artist
- 2004 Favorite Contemporary Inspirational Artist

American Music Awards—Nominations

- 2017 Favorite Contemporary Inspirational Artist
- 2015 Favorite Contemporary Inspirational Artist
- 2010 Favorite Contemporary Inspirational Artist
- 2008 Favorite Contemporary Inspirational Artist
- 2004 Favorite Contemporary Inspirational Artist
- 2003 Favorite Contemporary Inspirational Artist

ASCAP Christian Music Awards—Wins

- 2016 Song of the Year—"Flawless"
- 2016 Most Performed Song—"Flawless"
- 2015 Most Performed Song—"Greater"
- 2014 Most Performed Song—"You Are I Am"
- 2013 Most Performed Song—"The Hurt & The Healer"
- 2012 Most Performed Song—"Move"
- 2011 Songwriter/Artist of the Year
- 2011 Song of the Year—"All of Creation"
- 2011 Most Performed Song—"All of Creation," "Beautiful"
- 2010 Most Performed Song—"All of Creation"
- 2009 Most Performed Song—"God With Us," "You Reign"
- 2008 Most Performed Song—"Bring the Rain," "Hold Fast"
- 2007 Most Performed Song—"So Long Self"
- 2006 Most Performed Song—"Homesick," "In the Blink of an Eye"
- 2005 Most Performed Song—"Here with Me"
- 2004 Songwriter of the Year (Bart Millard)
- 2004 Most Performed Song—"I Can Only Imagine," "Spoken For," "Word of God Speak"
- 2003 Songwriter of the Year (Bart Millard)
- 2003 Most Performed Song—"I Can Only Imagine"

ASCAP Rhythm & Soul Music Awards—Wins

- 2014 Top Gospel Song—"I Can Only Imagine" (Tamela Mann's cover recording)

GMA Dove Awards—Wins

- 2017 Artist of the Year
- 2017 Pop/Contemporary Album of the Year—*Lifer*
- 2017 Songwriter of the Year (Artist)—Bart Millard

- 2005 Pop/Contemporary Album of the Year—*Undone*
- 2005 Special Event Album of the Year—*The Passion of the Christ: Songs*
- 2004 Song of the Year—"Word of God Speak"
- 2004 Artist of the Year
- 2004 Group of the Year
- 2004 Pop/Contemporary Song of the Year—"Word of God Speak"
- 2002 Song of the Year—"I Can Only Imagine"
- 2002 Pop/Contemporary Recorded Song of the Year—"I Can Only Imagine"
- 2002 Songwriter of the Year (Bart Millard)

GMA Dove Awards—Nominations
- 2017 Artist of the Year
- 2017 Song of the Year—"Even If"
- 2017 Songwriter of the Year (Artist)—Bart Millard
- 2017 Pop/Contemporary Album of the Year—*Lifer*
- 2017 Pop/Contemporary Recorded Song of the Year—"Even If"
- 2016 Christmas Album of the Year—*MercyMe It's Christmas!*
- 2016 Song of the Year—"Flawless"
- 2015 Artist of the Year
- 2015 Contemporary Christian Artist of the Year
- 2015 Song of the Year—"Greater"
- 2011 Group of the Year
- 2011 Pop/Contemporary Song of the Year—"All of Creation"
- 2011 Song of the Year—"All of Creation"
- 2009 Group of the Year
- 2009 Song of the Year—"You Reign"
- 2009 Country Album of the Year—*Hymned Again* (Bart Millard)

- 2008 Song of the Year—"Bring the Rain"
- 2007 Group of the Year
- 2007 Pop/Contemporary Album of the Year—*Coming Up to Breathe*
- 2006 Group of the Year
- 2006 Country Recorded Song of the Year—"Mawmaw's Song" (Bart Millard, Barry Graul)
- 2006 Inspirational Album of the Year—*Hymned* (Bart Millard)
- 2005 Group of the Year
- 2005 Artist of the Year
- 2005 Pop/Contemporary Album of the Year—*Undone*
- 2005 Special Event Album of the Year—*The Passion of the Christ: Songs*
- 2005 Long Form Music Video—*MercyMe LIVE*
- 2004 Artist of the Year
- 2004 Group of the Year
- 2004 Song of the Year—"Word of God Speak"
- 2004 Pop/Contemporary Song of the Year—"Word of God Speak"
- 2004 Songwriter of the Year (Bart Millard)
- 2004 Male Vocalist of the Year (Bart Millard)
- 2004 Children's Music Album of the Year—*I Can Only Imagine: Lullabies for a Peaceful Rest*
- 2003 Artist of the Year
- 2003 Group of the Year
- 2003 Song of the Year—"Spoken For"
- 2003 Pop/Contemporary Song of the Year—"Spoken For"
- 2002 Song of the Year—"I Can Only Imagine"
- 2002 Pop/Contemporary Recorded Song of the Year—"I Can Only Imagine"
- 2002 Songwriter of the Year (Bart Millard)

K-LOVE Fan Awards—Nominations

- 2017 Artist of the Year
- 2017 Group or Duo of the Year
- 2016 Song of the Year—"Flawless"
- 2016 Group or Duo of the Year
- 2015 Artist of the Year
- 2015 Song of the Year—"Greater"
- 2015 Group or Duo of the Year
- 2014 Artist of the Year
- 2014 Group or Duo of the Year
- 2013 Artist of the Year
- 2013 Group or Duo of the Year

MercyMe's Community Contributions

World Vision (2017–Present)

Mission Statement: World Vision is an international partnership of Christians whose mission is to follow our Lord and Savior Jesus Christ in working with the poor and oppressed to promote human transformation, seek justice, and bear witness to the good news of the Kingdom of God.

MercyMe's newest partnership is working alongside World Vision to enable children, their families, and their communities to build a better future for themselves. World Vision works to transform impoverished communities, provide emergency relief, improve access to quality education, promote justice and change unjust social structures, provide tools and support to gain access to nutritious food, provide accessible clean drinking water, and more. Both MercyMe and World Vision are committed to the body of Christ and follow Jesus' example in working alongside the poor and oppressed.

Compassion International (2003–2017)

Mission Statement: Releasing children from poverty in Jesus' name. In response to the Great Commission, Compassion International exists as an advocate for children, to release them from their spiritual, economic, social, and physical poverty and enable them to become responsible and fulfilled Christian adults.

Over a thirteen-year partnership with Compassion International, more than forty-three thousand children were sponsored, and $2 million was raised for the medical fund that ensures children receive vital immunizations, lifesaving treatments against deadly diseases, and prescribed therapeutic feeding. This equates to supplying fifty thousand dental kits (toothbrushes, toothpaste, dental checkups, and cavity treatments) or paying for HIV/AIDS care for eighty thousand patients (HIV testing, antiretroviral therapy, and ongoing care). Additionally, $1.1 million was raised for child survival programs, where thousands of impoverished mothers deliver healthy infants, and babies survive their first critical days and months of life. This equates to supporting forty-four child survival program centers for one full year of operation, serving more than three thousand mothers and babies.

Imagine A Cure (2008–2011)

Bart Millard's oldest son, Sam, was diagnosed with juvenile diabetes at the age of two, and Bart was determined to help find a cure. MercyMe founded the organization "Imagine A Cure," which existed to create financial, physical, and spiritual support for children and families affected by type 1 diabetes. In 2008, Bart Millard released a solo project called *Hymned Again*. With every purchase made on iTunes, a portion of the proceeds went to "Imagine A Cure." Subsequently, MercyMe folded "Imagine A Cure" and transferred their efforts to Compassion International's medical fund.

The Go Foundation (2003–2005)

Based on their 2003 tour "The Go Show," which played fifty cities in front of nearly 140,000 people and sold out twenty-five shows, MercyMe, along with Christian band Audio Adrenaline, created "The Go Foundation." Its purpose was to connect people who desired to go on mission trips with organizations that facilitated them. The organizations partnered with "The Go Foundation" were: International Mission Board, iWitness Ministries, International Commission, Awe Star Ministries, Spoken For Ministries, Student Evangelism with the North American Mission Board, East West Ministries International, International Sports Federation and G.O. Ministries Inc. More than five thousand people signed up to go on mission trips through the foundation.

ACKNOWLEDGMENTS

Thanks to:

Mom—You've endured so much to come out the amazing person you are. You're quite possibly the strongest person I know. And when you have days where you wrestle with not being there for me, understand you were there more than you know. My ability to sing came from you. My ability to persevere came from you. My ability to see the good in others came from you. The way my heart breaks for others came from you. And most importantly, my love for Tex-Mex came from you! I love you and am proud to call you Mom.

Stephen—You know me like nobody else. I have looked up to you my entire life and still do. For example, we've both had every reason not to be good fathers, yet the way you love your kids and the way they love you back have set the standard for what I want to be as a father. I am so grateful that God gave me you as my big brother. Well, I guess, technically, he gave you *me* as a little brother, since you were here first. So you should probably be thanking God for me. See what I did there?

My bandmates—You guys have literally been through it all with me, from me messing everything up to getting a couple of things right. And I cannot imagine this journey with anyone else. That goes for you, too, Jim.

My kids—I love you more than you will ever know! The three most important things *ever* to happen to me are meeting Jesus, marrying Mommy, and having you five! Every day I am astounded by who you already are . . . *and you're just getting started*! I will cheer you on as long as there is breath in my lungs. I love you, Sam. I love you, Gracie. I love you, Charlie. I love you, Sophie. I love you, Miles.

Shannon—My wife, my best friend, my rock. I've always said on stage, "I don't buy flowers for my wife to remind myself to love her; I do it because she's seen me at my absolute worst, and she still loves me." Thank you for not giving up on me. The day you said "I do," you said it not only to me but to the twenty-eight miles of baggage I carried with me . . . *and you still said yes*! I didn't think it was possible, but even after twenty years of marriage, I adore you more and more every day I am with you. I love you, friend.

ABOUT THE AUTHORS

BART MILLARD is a founding member and the lead singer of the multi-platinum-selling contemporary Christian band MercyMe. He is married to his childhood sweetheart, Shannon. They reside in Franklin, Tennessee, along with their children, Sam, Gracie, Charlie, Sophie, and Miles.

ROBERT NOLAND has authored more than seventy-five titles spanning across children, youth, and adult audiences over the past twenty-five years. He is an author, writer, editor, and project manager for Christian publishers, ministries, and faith-based organizations. He lives in Franklin, Tennessee, with his wife of thirty-plus years and has two adult sons. Visit robertnoland.com.

New from
Bart Millard
from MercyMe

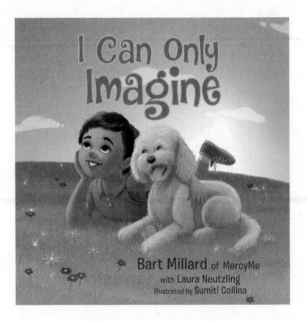

Available March 2018

Picture book ISBN: 9781400321339
Also available in board book ISBN: 9781400322015

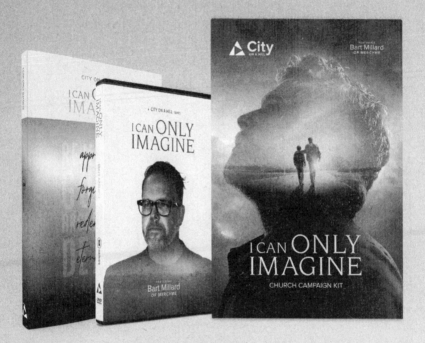